TEEN SENSE

(A Guide to the Turbulent Teens)

by

David Edens, M.A., Ph.D.

Warner Press
Anderson, Indiana

Printed in the United States of America

Contents

To my teen-age daughters
Deena and Debra
teachers of the art of child development
who in the process have put
gray hairs in my head
bills in my pocket
illustrations in my lectures
happiness in my home
and pride in my heart

Preface

Today's teen-age generation is hot copy for mass media. We read about "the alienated generation," "the radical ones," "the generation gap," "the riotous students," and most recently "the tuned-out generation." None of these epithets tend to give assurance to the anxious teen-ager trying to cope with a trying new phenomenon: adolescence!

The writer asked a group of young teen-agers to respond to the open-ended phrase, Being a teen-ager is like . . . Some of the descriptive responses were: "trying to build a fire with wet wood"; "a lobster being boiled alive"; "getting into new clothes that are too big and stiff"; "being put in a beef grinder"; "being in a fun house and not being able to get out"; "a little drop of water in a big sea"; "a race—always trying to catch up and always trying to make people think you're going to win"; and "falling into a deep, dark hole and grabbing for sticks you can't quite reach to help you climb higher."

But there is encouragement! This phase in your growing up is a combination of subtle and divine forces that are preparing you to cut the psychological umbilical cord which holds you dependent on your parents. You are venturing out from under your emotional roof. Call it advanced weaning. Later, after the adolescent campaign of parent rejection has achieved its purpose, you will recognize the value of parental guidance.

Much of what we are hearing and seeing suggests some definite and disturbing characteristics of this new mystique we label adolescence. The professional literature talks of a distinct teen-age subculture but appears to be in disagreement as to whether it actually exists. But separate culture or not, you will find it helpful in understanding and handling your teen-age years to know and recognize some of the normal physical, emotional, and spiritual manifestations of this age span.

—David Edens

1

The Big Transition

"I'm sure there's something wrong with Joe," an anxious mother told her doctor. "He used to be so active and interested in everything. All he does lately is lie around the house. He isn't interested in the ball games, his schoolwork, or even his friends. He stopped everything all at once. He eats constantly but doesn't have any energy. Will you give him a thorough examination so we'll know what's wrong with him?"

After examining and talking with Joe, the doctor's suspicions of a "rapid growth spurt" in this young teen-age boy were verified.

"Sometimes young teen-agers have to take time out to grow physically," explained the doctor. "Your son who was mentally, socially, and physically very active a few months ago is experiencing rapid bodily growth. You've noticed the difference lately."

"I should say!" interrupted the mother. "Joe doesn't have a pair of pants that aren't too short."

In the remaining minutes of the office visit, the doctor explained that teen-agers undergo many bodily changes.

TEEN SENSE!

WHAT'S HAPPENING?

Rapid growth accompanying organic changes may mean you have to yield the usual energy you expend in sports, social activities, even schoolwork, to the demand your body makes for energy. You eat more. You sleep more. You're easily upset emotionally. You have less motivation and interest in the world around you.

All other phases of your development may have to step aside while your body catches up or surges ahead in growth. When the body has been fed, rested, and given the attention it demands, it begins to release energy it can share. In a few months you probably will pick up the interests and activities you had to shelve for awhile.

Both Joe and his mother left the doctor's office with a better understanding of what had happened to Joe—a perfectly healthy body experiencing some normal hurdles in his race to physical manhood.

Since you tend to change in physical size and shape, sometimes at an alarming rate, it takes a little time to make your body work smoothly. During this transition period you tend to look less graceful than you did as a child. So, adolescence is sometimes referred to as "the awkward stage." However, the physical skills of an adolescent are much superior to a child, even though the awkward movements may seem to disprove this.

Some adolescents *are* more awkward than they were as children but this may be because of a critical attitude on the part of some parents, teachers, and neighbors that leads to self-consciousness and embarrassment. Thus, adolescence *as such* is not always what brings about awkwardness. Criticism from people close to you helps do it too.

Accompanying many bodily changes are new feelings, new boy-girl attractions, new reactions. You often have mixed feelings about what is happening to you and how to handle the situations. You have that new-old feeling. One adolescent expressed his feelings this way: "I'm not what I ought to be, I'm not what I'm going to be, but I'm sure not what I used to be!" And that's true. You are changing. You may feel unsure about the sexual side of life. Most people are confused about their standards of behavior. It's hard to know with certainty what is right and wrong today. Few responsible persons can tell you definitely what is expected and what is forbidden, and why.

NOW THERE'S A REASON

For a few years boys are a swift pain in your neck—if you're a girl. Boys put caterpillers down girls' backs. They skate faster than girls and jeer at them about it. They'd never let girls play on their baseball team. A girl can hardly see any purpose in these big, sloppy, rough, uncouth creatures.

Now, suddenly, the reason for boys and girls hits us. How can we date without each other? And what magic has transformed that gawky, long-legged, freckled-faced redhead into the coolest guy in town? Has he read Emily Post and Ann Landers? Or convinced his parents to buy him an electric guitar? Or is it simply that he's older, and she's older, and nature works in odd ways with odd wads?

TEEN SENSE!

Sooner or later you will have to answer the question, What am I looking for on a date? You say, "Why's that important? Just date, that's all." The question is important for one big reason: people tend to marry the persons they date. If we have no lifetime goals and values in our lives, we more than likely will settle for some second-rate character. If we date for the wrong reasons, we marry for the wrong reasons.

Henry Bowman, who made a ten-year study of divorce, concluded by saying divorce wasn't due so much to marriage failure as to courtship failure. If the divorcing couple had had the right kind of courtship, they would have discovered they did not have the common interests, common ideals, common religion, and common background which tend to assure marriage success.

From discussions with young people, several factors stand out, most of which apply equally to both girl and boy on a date. First are physical cleanliness, appropriate dress, and neatness of appearance. No Joe wants to date a Jill who hasn't had a bath for a week and whose hair is uncombed. The care of the body is important.

We expect our dates to be interesting conversationalists. This means that a date is a good listener and also can talk, at least at times, with interest and enthusiasm.

Of course, some young people talk too much. They feel compelled to keep up persistent "chatter," which also spoils the date.

One of the most important single events in adolescent development occurs in the changes that take place in the young person's body. Before these changes occur the adolescent *is* a child. After they have occurred the young person can *have* a child. Our bodies are gifts from God to be used for purposes in harmony with his will.

A physician in Austin, Texas, whose wife had been dead sixteen years, had done a superb job rearing his daughter. When asked how he had done this, he replied, "Well, I just said to her, 'You have one body,' and then I told her what it was for, that it had a purpose—a high purpose. And then I told her, 'Don't ever use anything God has given you for less than that for which it was made.' So far as I know, that's the way she lives."

You have a purpose—to use everything, even your body, which God has given you for its highest accomplishment.

WHAT IS ADOLESCENCE?

Many people think adolescence should be spelled "addle-essence." They believe the dominant mood during this period is to be addled. Addle-essence is a most trying time in a " 'tween-ager's" life, because it is then that you balance precariously between childhood and maturity. This is normal, a healthy sign of growth.

Adolescence usually is thought of as the stage between childhood and adulthood. Saying just when this stage begins and ends is difficult for so many factors must be considered. For example, certain obvious physical changes occur at this time but some of these changes are not really complete until well past the age of eighteen. Then, too, many adolescents are quite adult-like in some ways at fifteen or sixteen, while some adults continue to act like adolescents all their lives.

TEEN SENSE!

Since the adolescent's emotional behavior is often unpredictable and violent, some people have thought of the stage as one of "storm and stress." The feeling exists that adolescence is a time of great emotional upheaval through which every young person must pass. Many young people, however, reach maturity without any feeling of having come through an ordeal. Adolescence *can* be trying but it *need not* be. It can be fun.

The term *adolescence* is used in this book to denote a period during which the growing person makes the transition—spiritually, mentally, physically—from childhood to adulthood. Adolescence may be viewed as beginning roughly when young people begin to show signs of puberty. The stage continues until most youths are sexually mature, have reached their maximum growth in height, and have approximately reached their full mental growth as measured by intelligence tests. The period includes the years within the age range of twelve to the early twenties.

The real question during this time is how you feel about yourself and as a result how you conduct yourself. The Apostle Paul gave young Timothy some good advice along these lines:

"Don't let people look down on you because you are young; see that they look up to you because you are an example to them in your speech and behavior, in your love and faith and sincerity. . . . Give your whole attention, all your energies, to these things, so that your progress is plain for all to see. Keep a critical eye both upon your own life and on the teaching you give, and if you continue to follow the line I have indicated you will not only save your own soul but the souls of many of your hearers as well" (1 Tim. 4:12-16, Phillips).

During the teen-age years your values are becoming more precise. You are more aware of rules and religious codes. Your spiritual ideas are more similar to those of your parents now. To make the big transition successfully you need to understand what is taking place in your body and mind. Three basic changes are going on during this time: physical, social, emotional.

PHYSICAL CHANGES

Physical changes in adolescence are startling. Height and weight increase remarkably. Some boys shoot up six inches in one year. Rapid growth increases the appetite which often is satisfied through soft drinks, sundaes, and in-between snacks. Glands in the skin are changing to meet new demands, but the adolescent body is not always able, at the same time, to deal with both an increase in food *and* a strange diet. The result may be a breaking out with distasteful skin blemishes.

Not only do individual changes come about in body proportions but in fatigue, hunger, adjustability, and rate of basal metabolism (the chemical changes in living cells by which energy is provided for vital processes). These changes do not happen at the same time, age, or rate of speed in all adolescents. Teen-agers may be either early or late maturers. This fact explains the big hulk of a boy who may be physically mature but in other ways very childish. Such a boy cannot be expected to act like a grown-up just because he is ahead of himself physically.

13

TEEN SENSE!

Similarly, the young girl who is small and underdeveloped for her age may at the same time be emotionally or socially quite mature. Other adolescents her own age, however, may see her as a child.

Physical changes are important and may affect the way we feel about ourselves.

SOCIAL CHANGES

Powerful new emotions are developing. In early childhood boys and girls seem to recognize no sex differences in playing together—either sex is attractive for companionship. From the beginning of school to the beginning of adolescence, however, boys turn to boys for friends, and girls relate to girls. At adolescence another change takes place: boys and girls begin to seek partners from the opposite sex—a partner who soon is seen as something more than a companion, more romantic, more exciting. Thus the adolescent faces a new situation and is swept along with powerful new emotions which he is not certain he can control.

Little wonder, then, that the adolescent often is insecure and shows this by loud, brash talk or moodiness. He seems to enjoy meaningless chit-chat (because what is said is not as important as being with the gang). He vigorously tries to establish his importance, and avoids even minor social blunders. This behavior, while aggravating to the adult, is the adolescent's way of becoming familiar with the opposite sex and is a working-through period of greatest importance.

THE BIG TRANSITION

EMOTIONAL CHANGES

The adolescent, like the child, tends to respond emotionally in all-or-none fashion. When you are blue, you are *blue,* and when you are happy, you are on top of the world. However, this extreme response is more upsetting to you than to the child, for you feel that you should have better control. You try to hold in these strong emotional feelings to act more maturely (and also to prove your independence by keeping your feelings to yourself).

Intense concentration on your emotions often leads to moodiness, and sometimes to a kind of apathy. Without approving outbursts, parents can help by being sympathetic during the ups-and-downs. Also they can respect your desire to keep things to yourself, while at the same time making it clear that you can confide in them whenever you feel the need.

You may not say so, but you often welcome limits set by adults. Rules such as restricting the length of phone calls, no dating on certain days, and a curfew hour for dates, still leave you plenty of scope to make independent decisions.

The big transition is made when you mature physically, socially, and emotionally. Hopefully, in the chapters that follow are some guidelines which will be good teen sense.

2

Who Makes Up Your Mind?

Mass media is beaming much of its advertising thrust to teen-agers today. Why? Because this is the money market. American teen-agers this year are expected to spend a total of $21 billion as compared to $11 billion in 1965. Nearly half of the population in the United States today is under the age of twenty-five. A quick glance at the magazine rack in almost any drugstore will confirm that the appeal is to the youth market.

Teen-age girls, who are now the chief target of the manufacturers' advertising, spend $25,000,000 a year on deodorants, $20,000,000 on lipsticks, and $9,000,000 on home permanents. Boys buy a certain hair tonic not for the simple purpose of keeping their hair in order, but to exert a magical power over another fellow's girl.

TEENS HAVE CHANGED

Today's teen-agers differ from previous generations in three major ways:

1. You are more affluent, have more money to spend on everything, and therefore are subjected to more com-

mercialism. The advertisers have convinced you as being a special group with special needs for special things. Padded bras are available to twelve-year-old girls. In the advertisements for cigarettes the appeals are geared primarily to the young. One soft drink makes its appeal exclusively to the younger generation.

2. Television has made you more sophisticated, has exposed you to worlds you could not otherwise know. Ninety-four percent of American homes have television. Millions of people, a large part of the population, spend every evening watching the tube. A survey disclosed that only 14 percent of slum homes in one large Eastern city took newspapers, but 100 percent had television sets. In one Mexican-American family, the father was temporarily unemployed because of surgery. The mother earned a meager wage, but they owned a small, second-hand television set. The seven children, from four to fourteen, watch their set three to four hours a day. In their near poverty, this family expressed the hope of buying a toy which was advertised for "only $9.95."

3. Your parents are now less authoritarian than parents have ever been before. Some parents may even fear their teen-agers. It is much more difficult for parents to be dogmatic, especially when their children are better educated than they are.

The communication between parents and children has lessened. In many families the teen-agers' problems are met mostly by ignoring them. The daughter tends to go out on dates much earlier than her mother did, putting on makeup and wearing hose before she is emotionally ready for the sexual dialogue that they imply.

TEEN SENSE!

Yet her mother, while often pushing her daughter into these activities in order to keep up with other daughters and other mothers, passes on to the daughter little of her own experience and its meaning. And the daughter's father, absorbed in his job or business, has all but vanished as a moral authority in the family. Yours is the generation vacuum that mass media of all sorts have rushed in to fill.

Through the printed word, television, radio, and movies, the images and desires of a teen-ager are at once standardized and distorted. Even a brand of toothpaste was advertised as increasing sex appeal. Mass media are aware of your sexual awakening and capitalize on it.

BEER BELONGS?

The following advertisement recently appeared in newspapers across the nation:

BEER—toast to America's economy. The brewing industry is a massive and dynamic part of the national economy. Each year it pours billions of dollars into commerce and government.

- $1.4 billion state and federal excise taxes.
- $3 billion to employees, suppliers, and distributors.
- $875 million in agricultural products and packaging materials. The brewing industry is a proud contributor to America's prosperity.

UNITED STATES BREWERS ASSOCIATION, INC., 915 Olive Street, St. Louis, Missouri 63101

Under these words was a picture of a housewife putting a six-pack in her grocery cart. This ad is the soft sell, the

WHO MAKES UP YOUR MIND?

United States Brewers Association's attempt to justify the existence of their product and to say that "beer belongs." The flip side of this record could tell another story in terms of national crime, tragic accidents, and heartaches caused by excessive use of alcoholic beverages. The alcoholics in the United States number 6.5 million and their numbers grow by 200,000 annually.

One thoughtful estimate of the cost of alcoholism (including wage losses, crime and delinquency, accidents, hospital and medical care) each year is $900,000,000. Alcoholism can truthfully be called America's "billion dollar hangover." Yet the financial costs are trivial compared with the heartache, suffering, and distress so many persons suffer as a result of alcohol.

Some television commercials are more harmful than the violent crime programs. The commercials say a boy can get a girl if he wears the right hair cream or the girl can get a boy if she brushes her teeth with the right toothpaste. Love and marriage involve much more than using the right products or chemical compounds.

"LIKE A CIGARETTE SHOULD"

Cigarette ads that equate companionship with smoking are another offender against your perspective. You get the impression that it is necessary to have a cigarette in order to have affection and friendship. Think of a boy of thirteen. He has healthy lungs, a strong heart, a good appetite. He can't wait to try his first cigarette. Before this day is over, approximately 4,500 youngsters will smoke their first cigarette. This is true every day of the year. It adds up to a million and a half new young smokers annually.

TEEN SENSE!

This is a frightening piece of information when you consider that the younger a person is when he starts to smoke, the greater are his chances of serious illness or death at an early age. Most youngsters who smoke, first try it in junior high. By the time they graduate from high school, half the nation's teen-agers are smokers.

What the cigarette advertisements do not mention are the facts that people who smoke are more likely to die prematurely, in their forties and fifties, and even earlier, than those who do not smoke. Smokers are 1,000 percent more likely to die of lung cancer, 500 percent more likely to die of bronchitis or emphysema, 70 percent more likely to die of coronary heart disease. People who smoke have more chronic illness, lose more time from work, spend more time sick in bed, than those who have never smoked.

How do these facts, brought out by the Advisory Committee to the Surgeon General in their report, *Smoking and Health,* pertain to the youth of this country?

Because today's teen-agers are starting to smoke at a relatively early age, their risk of illness and premature death is even greater than that of their parents, who may not have started smoking so soon. One million of today's teen-age population will be victims of lung cancer.

While still in their teens, young smokers may fall prey to such disabling illnesses as heart ailments, bronchitis, emphysema, sinusitis, and peptic ulcer. Even before these ailments are diagnosed, youngsters may experience shortness of breath, annoying coughs, loss of stamina.

To put it bluntly, what has previously been considered a minor indulgence is now known to be a major cause of disease and death.

WHO MAKES UP YOUR MIND?

Undoubtedly, you are influenced by magazine and newspaper advertising which presents smokers as the gay, popular sophisticates you wish to emulate. To counteract the one-sided mass media, the American Association of Tuberculosis and Respiratory Diseases prepared a factual report about the dangers of smoking. One of their spot announcements on television and radio ends with the phrase: "It's a matter of life and breath." The American Cancer Society claims that smoking takes 8.3 years off one's life.

Pressure on the teen-ager from his friends is strong. Those first to exhibit so-called adult habits, such as smoking, are admired as swingers. To smoke in defiance of school or parental regulations may give them status.

ADULTS APPEAR CHILDISH

On television, too many adults are made to appear childish. For example, there's a commercial in which a lovable old man bets, loves, and then grabs another potato chip from a small child. He should have controlled himself. Ads that make apes out of parents and smart alecks out of children ought to be barred.

Just as cigarette advertisements are not likely to add to longevity, immature advertisements do not contribute to mental health. In one commercial a man runs wild to get some gooey candy bars, while seductive voices urge him to "give in, to the taste . . ." After such indulgence he won't stay in running condition for long. While the father may only gain weight, his child, following some other urge, may lose character. Unlike many adults, children are easily influenced. They become what they live. They absorb experience, assimilate it, and make it part of their personality. It is important, therefore, that what you experience be consistent with the adult's best values.

For the commercial advertisers, youngsters are a perfect target. They are suggestible and gullible. They learn jingles with amazing ease and are only too happy to oblige the announcer and pester their parents with sales slogans. "This fabulous toy is *only* $19.95. Every boy and girl should have it."

Child-care experts are divided in their opinions about the effects of television on teen-agers' personality or value development. But on one fact they all agree. Television and radio consume a significant part of a young person's day. Often, more of his time is spent with the TV set than with his father or mother. Even if the spectacles of sex and brutality were innocent fun, they would keep youngsters from more constructive activities.

For proper perspective, we can focus on the admonition which Paul gave the Christians at the church at Philippi: "Finally, brethren, whatsoever things are true, whatsoever things are honest, whatsoever things are just, whatsoever things are pure, whatsoever things are lovely, whatsoever things are of good report; if there be any virtue, and if there be any praise, think on these things" (Phil. 4:8). This verse presents adequate criteria for evaluating our thinking and conduct in the light of some of the ideas presented by the mass media.

SECURITY VERSUS INDEPENDENCE

A sixteen-year-old young person was asked to write a response to the question, How will an understanding of the forces at work in my struggle for independence help me become a more mature person?

His response was: "The teen-ager is most often seeking independence from parental discipline while at the same time trying to retain parental support—financially and environmentally. If a cooperative atmosphere is attained, the teen-ager can be allowed to set his own curfew, select personal friends, and so forth. In so doing, he must be able to assume the responsibility for his actions.

"In this manner he soon learns what maturity is. He appreciates the trust the parents have in him and most often will consider it his responsibility to maintain that trust."

EARNING RESPONSIBILITY

Probably your most important achievement is taking over from your parents complete responsibility for controlling how you should act. Your parents should gradually give you greater responsibility as you show you are able to assume it. In practice this seldom works smoothly. You may feel supremely confident that you can "take care of yourself" socially, emotionally, and financially—at least, in the disposal of money. In early adolescence this is not the case. Parents either tend to restrict you until they feel certain you are ready, or they give you your desired freedom only to find you bewilderedly returning for advice and help that you earlier spurned.

Two things are necessary at this point. *Parents* need to realize that they cannot make a man out of their boy unless they are willing to take the risk and give him a chance to test his abilities by himself. *Youth* need to realize that the best way to gain independence is to prove themselves by displaying a real sense of responsibility.

To illustrate: Sooner or later, the teen-ager will have to be given the family car to drive according to his own judgment. Only when you are freely allowed to do this can certain elements of maturity be claimed. On the other hand, in order to gain this privilege, be willing to go through an apprenticeship by repeatedly showing your parents you can be trusted to behave sensibly and reliably.

Proverbs 22:6 says: "Train up a child in the way he should go, and when he is old, he will not depart from it." What does this verse mean to you?

Parents have responsibility for guiding and training the child, but the child has his own rate and development of growth—"the way *he* should go."

BEHAVING LIKE THE GROUP

The adolescent's insecurity leads to conformity—that is, behaving just like the others in his group. While this also can be seen in children and adults, it generally is thought that conformity in adolescence has a somewhat different quality.

The child, for example, appears to want to conform to an individual (perhaps some currently popular football or baseball star), or to a style of dress, or a way of talking, mainly because he wants to be like that particular *individual*—and he tends to feel this identification strongly. The adult, on the other hand, conforms because he wishes to identify with a particular group of people—and so dresses in their fashion.

24

WHO MAKES UP YOUR MIND?

Adolescent conformity seems to combine the intensity of feeling of the child with the aims and attitudes of the adult. The adolescent, in his struggle to achieve independence from adults, sticks closely to friends of his own age. This makes you feel secure as you rebel against the authority of grown-ups. This sometimes passionate need to conform to the gang is extremely important to you and should be understood and tolerated by parents so long as your activities are not dangerous or offensive.

SOME GUIDEPOSTS TO MATURITY

Most humans reach physical maturity by the age of twenty-one. People take for granted that such maturity will be attained. However, we may question whether anyone's social, emotional, or spiritual behavior can ever be considered entirely mature at all times. Striving to attain the goal set by Christ to "be ye therefore perfect" in all these areas is a constant challenge.

Certain guideposts may help. The socially and emotionally mature individual is one who can: (1) make independent decisions based on the help and advice available; (2) accept responsibility for these decisions; (3) postpone immediate gratification of needs until richer satisfaction may be gained; (4) give, as well as accept, friendship; (5) develop a saving sense of humor.

When you have reached the stage where these reactions become habitual, you gain self-confidence and will be regarded by others as mature.

The struggle between security and independence must be seen in light of ethical choices. The process of making up our minds put us in tension with these choices.

25

3

Everybody Needs Somebody Somehow

Let us ask two penetrating questions: Who has more influence on us *now*—our parents or our friends? Whose approval do we value the most? These questions are difficult for everyone to answer. Many factors are involved. We all have need of parental guidance and we all like to be a significant member of our own age group and have their approval.

One of the guideposts for maturity mentioned in the previous chapter was "give, as well as accept, friendship." We need friends and we need to be a friend. No one is an island unto himself.

YOU BE THE PARENT

Let us put ourselves in the mother's and father's position in the following situation. What are your reactions?

"My husband and I have always been active members of our church. We sincerely believe that going to church and keeping the Lord's Day adds something to our lives that is worth preserving and passing on to our children.

EVERYBODY NEEDS SOMEBODY SOMEHOW

"Our two girls—they are fifteen and sixteen—
have always gone willingly and with apparent satisfaction to the church youth activities. But during
the last year, they both have begun to rebel.

"It's true that many of their friends have
dropped out, and that makes it harder. But my
husband and I have never seen why we should
be lax just because other parents are. Now, however, the girls have backed each other in bringing
it to an open issue. They won't go unless we make
them. And if we insist, they say they will feel
like hypocrites.

"We are so concerned about their refusal that
it is impossible not to take it seriously. Yet, how
can we let them stop without betraying our trust
as parents? Isn't it our duty to our children to
maintain fine standards?"

In earlier life you were more concerned about what the
adults or those in authority thought. Now, probably, you
are more interested in the views of your friends or peers.
You do not want to be too far out of line with your gang.
You want to think, talk, and act as your friends do. You
have developed a group spirit and want to do as others of
the group are doing. Few things do you prize more than
to be accepted by your friends, and few misfortunes are
more devastating than to be rejected by those whose
friendship you desire.

This conformity involves language, clothes, customs,
and activities. The thoughts, feelings, and attitudes of the
peer group, sometimes outweighs personal ideas. To
have the approval of your friends is not the only important
thing. Your best friends are those who have ideals and
standards.

27

TEEN SENSE!

Some young people are so completely preoccupied with themselves, their wants, their own success or failure, their own opinions, that they shut others out entirely. They spend so much of their emotional energies on themselves that they have none left to aim at the more mature focus of life—others. If this were reversed, that is, if all emotional energies were spent on others, none would be left for self—but none would be needed. For full maturity we need to give, as well as accept, friendship.

Friends are found according to certain principles of social relationships. In general, teen-agers, like other persons, tend to find their friends where their interests are. They tend to associate with people who enjoy doing the things they themselves like to do. They feel most comfortable with those who share their way of life, pursue their values, and uphold their standards. This is the principle of homophily: the tendency of similar persons to like one another and to make friends within their own group rather than outside it.

Friends are important to us. With a close friend, we can share the confidences and raise the questions that arise out of our shared experiences. We learn to trust one another enough to be honest and open without pretending. We serve to reinforce one another in the values and standards we hold dear and to accept our differences without threat or pressure.

Most of all, close friends help us evaluate ourselves. We all stand in need of approval. A true friend can appraise our behavior and candidly comment on it. He can encourage us to keep up the good work or suggest areas in our lives that need changing. Real friends can critically examine mistakes, decide what went wrong, and advise how to handle the same situation the next time it comes up. Teen-agers go to close friends with problems in boy-girl relationships—real or potential.

PRESSURES OF THE GANG

How would you react to the following situation?

"Most of the boys and girls in our crowd have paired off. John, who is two years older than I (I am fifteen), has asked me to go steady with him. The idea does not attract me particularly since it could mean more petting and less chance to meet other boys. But it's the custom of the gang and if I say no, I'll be left out of many things. If I say yes, I can always be sure of a date even though it may not be the date I would always prefer."

Can a fifteen-year-old think through this problem? Increasingly broad opportunities are needed where teens can find themselves as socially acceptable, effective human beings.

A former dean at Colby College tells of a sophomore who came to him saying he was leaving college because of his poor academic performance. The dean asked the young man to send postcards back during his trip to California to look for a job, and expressed hope that he would soon return.

The student drove only twenty miles before turning back and going to the dean to say, "I've decided to stay. I didn't know anyone around here cared enough to ask for a postcard."

To have a friend is to be one. And doesn't everybody need somebody somehow?

4

Making Meaningful Decisions

When Jess Neely, dean of college football coaches, gave up his position at Rice University, he had served as a head coach for forty years. Prominent among the tributes given him was the statement: "He always emphasized fundamentals." Learning to make meaningful decisions is fundamental to each of us.

In our society, many people would advise us to "eat, drink, and be merry, for tomorrow we may die." The moral code of Ernest Hemingway is popular today: "What is moral is what you feel good after, and what is immoral is what you feel bad after."

Freedom to make decisions is one of life's greatest gifts. This freedom of decision is a liability as well as an asset. Often the decision is a difficult one. Temptation is a fork in the road.

The problems which we all face often differ. However, the choice between right and wrong is one which we face all our lives. The Christian can continually strive for perfect goodness, not by withdrawing from the world, but by fulfilling the duties of a Christian in every area of life. Because we do have to choose, we are constantly in need of help in making meaningful decisions.

THE JESUS ETHIC

Many persons have long held that the highest ethic comes from Jesus, and the best record of his life is in the Bible. Paul urged young Timothy to hold fast to his own tested doctrine, to remember who his teachers were, and also to remember the tradition of faith found in the sacred writings on which he had been nurtured as a child.

The well-rounded attitude toward religious truth is essential. Thus, we avoid mistaking a partial truth for the whole truth (which is fanaticism), and we escape the vagueness which makes religion a formless optimism based on no clear-cut doctrines (as in a certain type of liberalism or situation ethics).

Man strives to be "perfect" or complete, a whole man developed mentally and spiritually. In every case the reason for arrested development in Christian character is that somewhere we disobeyed the truth contained in God's Word. We refused to study, or failed to submit ourselves to the light that came to us through study. No advancement can be made until we obey the particular thing God says to us through his Word.

We stop growing because of something we know to stop doing but are still doing, or we refuse some call of truth. Realistically, we need to go back to the point of our disobedience and there obey. Some of us may have to tramp our way back to a point where we stood five years ago to find the place where our growth was stunted.

31

TEEN SENSE!

We can draw on the resources of our own Christian experiences and on God's Word for guidance in knowledge of right and wrong.

It seems obvious to most young people today that we are facing a moral crisis. No single authority guides our conduct. Teen-agers understand the "new morality" to say, in effect, "Dirty books are not dirty, swear words not profane, pornography is art, promiscuity is permissive, and agnosticism is open-mindedness." The teen-ager needs to come to an understanding and acceptance of a moral code consistent with the Christian faith.

The Bible does not always give us examples of specific behavior but it clearly sets forth principles by which we may judge. It labels dishonesty, selfishness, immorality, and greed as contrary to the nature of Christ and his followers. It warns against the consequences of evil in our lives. The Bible reminds us that no middle ground can exist. We either conform or we are transformed. We learn from the words of Jesus that, "Ye cannot serve God and mammon" (Matthew 6:24).

However, the Bible cannot serve as a good luck charm to keep evil away. Before the Bible can guide us, we must want help and be willing to receive it. Through reading the Bible regularly and applying its truths to daily life we can find the help we need.

The Ten Commandments, the Sermon on the Mount, the book of James, the letters of Paul, and other great passages of the Bible give unmistakable guidance in confronting specific issues of life. The examples of Joseph, Daniel, Stephen, and other Bible characters inspire us to godly living.

32

MAKING MEANINGFUL DECISIONS

The Bible, when loved and used, may become the standard by which we measure our lives, and thereby make meaningful decisions.

An important question is, "What should be my attitude when I realize I have made an unwise decision?"

The writer asked a teen-ager how she handled unwise decisions. She jestingly replied, "I cry a lot." Unfortunately, this is all some people know to do with unwise decisions. But a responsible person knows how to make decisions and accepts the consequences of his decisions.

THE CAN'T-HELP-ITS

All of us make decisions. The real test of our maturity comes in living with an unwise decision. For those who have not already discovered for themselves, no problem is more difficult than managing unwise decisions. The greatest temptation is to blame other people or circumstances for the poor decision and thus project the responsibility elsewhere. This process is known psychologically as rationalization. It never gets at problem solving because it evades the problem.

The lazy student may say he "flunked" because "My English teacher did not like me." The spoiled child might insist that neighborhood children pick on him, by claiming they are roughnecks. A poorly adjusted teen-ager blames her unhappiness on the fact that "My mother never really loved me," as if that ended the matter.

The assumption behind excuses we make for ourselves is that if we can discover alibis outside of ourselves we can escape responsibility for being the way we are. It is not our fault. Abraham Lincoln put it aptly when he explained the reputation of a village scoundrel by saying: "He's got the can't-help-its." The man was forever explaining his behavior in terms of people and things over which he had no control. Other people made him the way he was and he could not help it. The world is full of people who have "the can't-help-its." Persons who learn nothing from unwise decisions and find no means for growth in hurts brought upon themselves.

Three basic fallacies in our thinking make it relatively easy for us to escape responsibility for our decisions. We may hide behind the popular notion that "you can't change human nature." When you reduce that idea to its personal equation, the essence of it is: "I cannot change me." Therefore, it follows, "I can't help the decisions I made. I was born to lose."

So, if we are neurotic, strained by tension, frustrated, dishonest, failures, or anything else, we are a facsimile of plain human nature and we can't help it. We provide ourselves with a bulletproof excuse for staying precisely as we are. What is more, we rob life of meaning that comes from self-conquest. We must shoulder the responsibility for the decisions we make. Jesus said, "No man, having put his hand to the plough, and looking back, is fit for the kingdom of God" (Luke 9:62).

The second fallacy in our modern thinking is a refinement of the first. It is the curious but common notion that human nature being what it is, it is unfair to put character under strain. Editorial comment at the time of the West Point cheating scandal noted that putting a man on his honor not to cheat subjects him to terrific strain. Therefore, monitoring students during examinations is a better system. West Point officials were condemned roundly because they trusted in "the honor of the corps" and made it relatively easy for men to cheat.

Editorial writers seemed to be saying: It is all very well to have an honor system, but you had better relieve students of the unnecessary strain involved in being honest. You really cannot expect a man to be responsible for integrity if you tempt him. The students who cheated were dismissed from West Point. They made a bad decision and they had to suffer the consequences. Strain builds one person and destroys the other. Personality necessarily and inevitably is subjected to moral stress, but the outcome depends on something in the person.

The third fallacy in our thinking which enables us to run out on our responsibility for unwise decisions is the idea that character is merely the product of our environment. We simply "do as the Romans do" because it comes naturally and we cannot be expected to do anything else. The prophets of Israel, towering above their contemporaries in public thinking and private living, are the glory of Israel. The simple truth is that we can be better than our environment and nobler than our society.

FASHION FOR TRIUMPH

When we make an unwise decision can we take the stuff of which we are made and fashion it for triumph? Can we take our minds and our emotions and our wills and manage them with the wisdom of God? Or are we bound to run off the road into the ruts of misery and conflict?

TEEN SENSE!

At times we wonder. Wistfully and sadly we say when we make unwise decisions, "I wasn't myself when I did that," and it is true enough. With a bit of an ache in the heart we say, "I didn't mean to," as if our behavior ran off and left our intentions behind. Exasperated, we ask ourselves, "Now why did I do that?" as if some imp of perversity pushed us to folly when we were looking in the opposite direction.

The question of a small boy after he had been vigorously spanked is suggestive, "Mom," he asked tearfully, "how do you make yourself do what you ought to do?" That is the ultimate question, and we often dislike ourselves because we do not know the answer. Our experience leads us to a fundamental contradiction. On one hand, we are confronted by the obvious fact that we are responsible for ourselves, and on the other hand, we face the fact that we make unwise decisions.

How do we handle unwise decisions? The first and obvious starting point is to recognize that the decision was a poor one. This is half the battle. Now we must face who is involved or affected by the decision. We may need, as Jesus suggested, to go and be reconciled with our offended brother (see Matt. 5:23-24). This is not easy to do, but from a Christian point of view it may be necessary.

All of us need counsel from time to time. If you have made an unwise decision, talk it out. Don't bottle it up. The adage holds true that honest confession is good for the soul. Find some level-headed, understanding person and share your unwise decision with him. Prayer, sharing our concerns with God, may help us more realistically evaluate our decisions.

5

Upheaval in Value Systems

In the play, *Green Pastures,* one of the characters says, "De levees is gonter bust an' everything dat's fastened down is comin' loose."

We can apply this to our personal and world crises. We have new frontiers in space. We have left a world that had many things nailed down with a sense of security. In the winds that sweep our world, "everything dat's fastened down is comin' loose." Or so it seems.

Fears and doubts today pull out the nails of security. And the once orderly structure of life looks like so many loose ends, morally, as well as intellectually. We are un-anchored ships in the tempest of change.

Modern life in the United States is rich with value choices and opportunities, but life is also very confusing. It is far more difficult for a teen-ager to develop clear values today than it was in the simpler, more somber life of the turn of the century.

One major reason for this is the change in the family, where, many believe, values develop. In recent years, we have seen dramatic, if not frightening, changes in the family: working mothers (one out of three), broken homes (estimated at one out of five), and geographic mobility (about one family in five moves every year). Family sharing has decreased. The consequence of this upheaval in values may be a growing confusion in your life.

New approaches to making moral decisions have been introduced in recent years. Freedom to choose one's values is one of life's great blessings. However, it is not an unmixed blessing. It can be a liability as well as an asset. For with this freedom to choose goes the obligation of finally having to decide. The choice between right and wrong is one which we must continually face all our lives. Because we do have to choose, we are constantly in need of help in making decisions. This chapter discusses the strength and weakness of the current approaches to making moral decisions.

The two extremes of modern thinking on morality are *legalism* on the one hand and *relativism* on the other. Neither of these extreme positions meets the demands the Christian faith makes on personal and social conduct, nor do we discover authentic morality by charting the middle ground between the two.

Today the more popular of these two extremes, and the opposite of legalism, is relativism, also known as situational ethics or the new morality. One form of the new morality is the current rebellion against legalism and Puritanism. The new morality claims the highest ethical insight as its justification, and it, therefore, deserves our understanding, whether we want to give it allegiance or not.

UPHEAVAL IN VALUE SYSTEMS

One of the best evaluations of the new morality is found in Kyle Haselden's book, *Morality and the Mass Media* (Broadman Press, 1968).

The new morality holds that the test of love has to be applied to each isolated event of life as the sole test of good or evil. If the behavior meets the test of love, it is good. If not, it is bad. Thus all laws, rules, commandments, and codes are thrown out.

One thing alone—what love demands of the moment and what the moment demands of love—determines the rightness or wrongness of human conduct. Thus, right and wrong are determined by the situation and not by some eternal and absolute law. According to this belief no moral rules can be prepared for life's expected or surprising events. No laws that we have been taught from our youth up—so the new morality says—are absolutely binding under all possible situations.

The new moralists say it is possible under certain circumstances that the love we have learned in Jesus may demand that we lie, steal, kill, commit adultery. These circumstances may be rare, but they can occur. For by this theory, there are no absolute, universal, changeless moral imperatives which might not somewhere at sometime bow to the superior demands of love. This view is documented by one of the spokesman for the new morality—Joseph Fletcher. He writes in one of his books, *Moral Responsibility* (Westminster Press, 1967, p. 14): "Hence in such Christian ethics nothing has any worth except as it helps or hurts persons, either human or divine—God or neighbor or self. Good and evil are intrinsic. Right and wrong, depend upon the situation."

TEEN SENSE!

Fletcher makes it plain that his "anything" includes theft, lying, fornication, and murder. All of these he indicates, can be not merely necessary evils, but positive goods. But what of rape, incest, cruelty to little children? Even here, he leaves open the possibility that these normally vile human relations may in some situations be positively good. The new morality moves from values to behavior without the structures of standards, codes, or rules.

The trouble with the new morality is that in its preoccupation with people it appears to be unprincipled and therefore permissive. One can get away with any kind of behavior if he can call it love. This view of ethics is so easily distorted into an excuse for immorality—especially into sexual permissiveness—that its popularity with large numbers of high school and college-age students is easily understood.

LEGALISM

Another value system is legalism. Christian legalism assumes that in the teachings of Jesus and his disciples, in the Ten Commandments, and in the church doctrines we have a detailed, inflexible, always appropriate, moral code which is adequate for all times, persons, and circumstances. All a Christian has to do is learn these rules and live by them.

The legalist lives as though Jesus had not come to set men free from bondage to the law. At his best and at his worst, the legalist is the rich young ruler saying, "All these have I observed"(Mark 10:20). Yet he knew, even before Jesus made the point, that he had an aching void in his letter-of-the-law life. And he went away sorrowful.

40

UPHEAVAL IN VALUE SYSTEMS

The legalist is the group of scribes and Pharisees who brought to Jesus a woman caught in adultery and said to him, "Master, this woman was taken in adultery, in the very act. Now Moses in the law commanded us, that such should be stoned: but what sayest thou?" (John 8:4-5). Then Jesus said, "He that is without sin among you, let him first cast a stone at her" (4:7). The legalists had to call it a day and drop their rocks.

Some people can live thoroughly consistent lives by the rules. You may know some. But, generally, legalism fails as authentic morality. Under legalism the important thing is that a man has obeyed a religious regulation; therefore, he gains another favorable mark. Jesus knew that adultery can be committed by a look, whether there is a physical act or not. He was concerned not only with the act but also with the thought and attitude of a person.

Legalism describes the good life in static, restrictive, negative terms. Authentic morality is the freedom into which life is invited by Jesus, rather than the restrictive no of a negative response.

Legalism tends to concentrate on trivialities. It causes one to major on the minors and forget the abundant life that Jesus came to give.

Finally, legalism precludes the working of the Holy Spirit. Paul said it "quenches the Spirit," and his letter to the Galatians is a denunciation of legalism.

DOES MORALITY RATE?

Only the uninformed person would deny that the Bible occupies an important place in our land. Attitudes toward the Bible vary from praise to superstitious awe to scorn, but seldom do we encounter anyone who rejects it altogether. The Bible continues to be a best seller, but it is more than that. Politicians frequently quote from the Bible. Dramatists and moviemakers exploit its themes. We take oaths with the Bible in hand. Brides carry the New Testament at their weddings. Pilots, soldiers, and others on dangerous missions frequently carry the Bible as part of their "equipment." The Bible has gone even to the moon.

Is it not strange that a book so highly honored could at the same time be so generally neglected? In some homes the Bible is prominently displayed and to place something on it or to mark it would be regarded as sacrilege. Yet it may never be opened and read. Christians have an awareness that somehow this book is unique. They believe the Bible is a sacred book. Therefore, it is reverenced, honored, respected, but seldom read and rarely understood.

From our practices we can realistically ask, does morality rate? What is the authority of the Bible? How can a book continue to be revered when it is increasingly neglected? What do you think of the following statements: The Bible is a dead book unless it is read by a living church. Likewise, the church is a dead institution unless it is corrected and reformed in every age by a living Bible.

Are the changing times in which we live making it increasingly difficult for us to understand this ancient classic? Is the difficulty explained by our busyness, our preoccupation with other things? Is the fault solely with us, or is there something about the Bible itself that contributes real barriers to understanding for us in this age?

UPHEAVAL IN VALUE SYSTEMS

No single answer can be given to these questions. Many factors contribute to confusion regarding the Bible. Interestingly, the Bible is not a book, but a library or collection of sixty-six books written over thirty generations, by over one hundred different writers. The Bible is made up of many different types of literature. It contains history, drama, poetry, and codified religious and civil law. The Bible contains songs, prayers, letters, and visions, as well as moral instructions and proverbs.

All the material in the Bible comes from ancient times. Moreover, the language, the customs, the way of thinking and expressing ideas springs from a culture very different from ours. All of these and many other factors contribute to modern man's difficulty with the Bible.

Before saying, "What's the use?" we should remember that these factors do not constitute impossible barriers to understanding and responding to the authority of the Bible. These factors simply mean that the Bible is to be studied, rather than just read.

Fortunately, we have advantages for studying the Bible that were denied our forefathers. We have more accurate and more readable translations and versions of the Bible to study. We have better aids to help us understand the history, the customs, and the background from which the Bible was written. And we have a vast library of commentaries to help us to see the material in context and to place it in historical perspective.

However, one of the major problems for the contemporary Christian as he approaches the Bible is his failure to discern what the whole work is really about. The authority of the Bible remains a mystery until it is seen as bearing unique and authoritative witness to what God himself was doing in the person of Jesus Christ. That God acted in Christ is the supreme authority of the Christian faith.

The Bible is unique, not because of its literary excellence, scientific assumptions, structure, and even its words, but because it is a living book that continues to speak and to affect our lives. The Bible brings us the exciting news that God in Christ lives among us and is victorious in our behalf.

The Bible bears witness to what God has done. Only in the Bible are we told what happened to prepare the way for Christ's coming. Only in the Bible can we find the claims Christ made for himself and also examine the claims that were made for him by other men. Nowhere else does the living Christ meet his people with such saving power. Jesus Christ is the unchanging Word supremely manifesting God's unchanging love for all men. As the primary witness to this truth, the authority of the Bible deserves a place no other book can share.

Quite honestly, what is the most perplexing problem you have encountered in studying and understanding the Bible? What efforts have you made to reconcile these perplexities with the church's claim that the Scriptures are unique and authoritative? In what ways do rapid cultural changes through which we are living raise new barriers to biblical understanding? In what ways do such changes open new opportunities for biblical understanding?

UPHEAVAL IN VALUE SYSTEMS

The following four statements are about the Bible. What would be some reactions to these statements?

1. Those who reverence the Bible but do not read it have no cause to criticize those who read and do not reverence. But those who read and do not reverence have cause to criticize as fake the reverence of those who do not read. Unbelievers may yet make honest men out of believers.

2. The Bible, unless it is understood carefully, can become a cruelly dangerous book. It is both the father of knowledge and the mother of superstition.

3. In the stories of the Old and New Testaments and supremely in the picture of God that dominates the entire Bible, Christians discover themselves alive and wanted.

4. Though often hidden behind intellectual difficulties, man's perplexity with the Bible is not primarily intellectual. Nor is it primarily moral. Fundamentally, it is religious. It is the perplexity of those who are uneasy in mind and conscience and soul, because they have never honestly faced the demand which God makes upon them.

Paul adequately expressed the nature of the Bible's authority when he said: "All scripture is inspired by God and profitable for teaching, for reproof, for correction, and for training in righteousness, that the man of God may be complete, equipped for every good work" (2 Tim. 3:16-17).

The Bible belongs to the whole world as does no other book. It is available in more than a thousand languages. Through the years Christians have affirmed that the Bible is the supreme authority for faith and practice.

45

6

Are Times Different?

Today's teen-agers are very aware of the whole world. Through TV they are plugged into the problem areas of the entire globe. Every day they are bombarded with cosmic no-nos.

"I sure get tired of my folks treating me like a kid," said Jack disgustedly as he, Bill, Ann, and Debra relaxed in the lunchroom. "It's 'Don't do this,' 'You're too young for that,' all day long. They have the idea that I'm not old enough to decide anything for myself."

"Yeah, I know how you feel," echoed Bill. "I can't have the car for a date because I'm too young. I'm old enough to have a driver's license, but the only time they let me drive is when dad or mom is along."

"You should talk," gasped Ann. "I have to be in at eleven on Saturday night, or I get grounded for a week. Who else has to get in that early?"

"My folks give me the third degree when I get in. 'Who were you with? What did you do? Where did you go?' You just can't have any privacy," added Debra.

ARE TIMES DIFFERENT?

Do these complaints have a familiar ring? Are times really different? What should be your attitude toward the authority of parents and older persons?

The Apostle Paul probably was not a parent, but he said a lot of wise things about family life. He said, "Children obey your parents in the Lord: for this is right. Honor thy father and mother" (Eph. 6:1-2). He also said, "And, ye fathers, provoke not your children to wrath: but bring them up in the nurture and admonition of the Lord" (Eph. 6:4). So we learn that children are to obey and honor their parents.

Parents should be gentle and patient with their children. If children do not obey and honor gentle and understanding parents, there is difficulty. But it is sadder still when children have to obey parents who are harsh and unkind. Let us put it into a formula: $OC+GP = GH$ (obedient children plus gentle parents equals good home). Sounds neat, doesn't it? But how do children and parents put this formula to work?

Perhaps we need to "lift the receiver" and listen to one another. Maybe we are the ones to begin use of the formula. Communication is always at the heart of problems of authority. Communication, whatever else it is, is always a two-way process. Parents want their children to come to them with their questions. Children may not always appreciate their parent's answers. Sometimes parents may be wrong, but they want to help.

Talking is not always communication. In some families a lot of talking goes on but no real exchange of warmth and understanding is felt. A big difference exists between the spontaneous conversation teen-agers enjoy and continuous chatter just to secure attention. A young person may talk continuously but say nothing that really matters. He may be using speech as a defense against prying questions, holding back his real feelings for fear his parents will not understand.

How can you prevent talk from becoming a barrier instead of a bridge? Good communication between parents is a foundation for communication between parents and children.

In a good home, channels of love and understanding are kept open at all times. Paul said, "Let not the sun go down upon your wrath: neither give place to the devil" (Eph. 4:26-27). In paraphrase, Paul was saying; "Never go to sleep with a quarrel in your heart. If you do, the devil is your roommate." Probably the six most difficult words in the family vocabulary are: "I was wrong. I am sorry."

We should try to keep the lines of communication open between us and our parents. And, if an honest look shows that the communications have become clogged with the derbis of everyday problems, we can do our best to open them again.

A teen-ager needs to feel free to seek advice from his parents. The parents' attitude usually determines the extent to which this freedom is used. Many parents have thought, *I wonder why my child never asks questions?* The answer may be that the teen-ager has been preconditioned by his parents' attitude.

If a teen-ager knows a parent is going to go into shock or explode in criticism before he even finishes talking, he soon learns to keep his problems, experiences, and feelings to himself. If a parent laughs at the teen-ager's confidences or repeats them to others, the confidences will stop. Parents must respect their teen-agers interests.

Family discussion periods can keep open the channels of communication between a teen-ager and his parents. Discussion periods afford an opportunity for teen-agers to ask the advice of parents. These discussions need not always focus on crises or big problems. At the dinner table, at times when friends or relatives are being entertained, many things can spark healthy discussions—neighborhood happenings, community affairs, items from newspapers.

Parents can broaden the topics, stimulate interest, and introduce some values about human nature. Teen-agers can learn to express themselves on subjects that do not come out of a textbook or a theme.

Families who are accustomed to talking with each other about nonfamily affairs—above the level of gossip—also usually will feel free to communicate with one another on personal matters. Communication is a necessity for teen-agers.

You must take the initiative in getting the advice you want. Try your parents first. But what if you feel that their judgment is not in your best interest? Then test it out elsewhere. An impartial adult can help you think clearly on an emotional matter. A counselor is trained to be objective. An understanding adult leader or teacher usually can see several sides to an issue and can give some insight which might not have occurred to you or your parents.

You should talk over problems with other adults if for some reason you do not feel you can confide completely in your parents. Who are these other adults? They may be your pastor, teacher, youth director, or school guidance counselor.

Many of the personal problems brought to these various persons stem from our changing world. People everywhere are beginning to recognize that it is as foolish to live indefinitely with a cultural or emotional distress, without trying to ease it, as it would be to ignore an aching tooth.

If you will take the initiative, you can find someone who will be most willing to hear you out and share the burdens of your heart. It's up to you.

Do you and your family operate on a partnership basis? Which of the following do you *sometimes* do and which do you *usually* do? Check yourself:

- I try to be cheerful at home.
- I try to see my parents as people who have problems of their own.
- I attempt to see my parents' point of view.
- I try to remember to tell my parents about my activities in which I feel they will be interested.
- I accept my share of the work around home, keeping my room and clothes in respectable order.
- I introduce my friends to my parents, and try to help them to know each other.
- I remind myself that other members of the family like to use the car and telephone, and need money.
- I worship God with my family, both at home and at church.
- I respect my family's privacy, as much as I expect them to respect my own privacy.

7

The Drag of Drugs

"Chaplain, we're all of the same faith here," remarked one of the patients at Riverside Hospital for the rehabilitation of adolescent narcotic users. "You see," he said, "Horse [heroin] is our god and the way we get a fix [shot of heroin] is our ritual. We're as hepped up about our religion as you are about yours." He smiled and added, "But I guess ours costs us a little more than yours."

The chaplain wondered if the patient referred to the high prices he had to pay for heroin or if he referred to the price he had to pay in terms of self-degradation, alienation, and helplessness which plague the addicted person. These are the wounds "that draw no blood," and as Isaiah says, "have not been closed, neither bound up, neither mollified with ointment."

The author of this book was that chaplain. I have counseled with teen-age drug users over the past twenty years. I've seen it from many sides and what I've seen has not been pleasant.

Drug abuse is many things. It is the heroin user injecting his bag of H, the Methedrine user high on "speed," the teen-ager smoking "pot," the twelve-year-old sniffing model-airplane glue. But it is also the adult starting his day with an amphetamine for a needed "pick-me-up" and ending it with several drinks to "unwind" and a barbiturate to put him to sleep.

The problem of drug abuse reaches deeply into our values, aspirations, and fears. It is an emotionally charged area for almost all of us. Drug abuse is a serious, growing problem here and in many other countries.

Much of the material in this chapter comes from the National Institute of Mental Health (NIMH) and incorporates the latest scientific findings on the drug scene.

Drug abuse, like other forms of deviant behavior, may have varying causes. For some users, it may represent ill-advised experimentation, for others, it may indicate basic psychological problems.

Drugs differ widely in their chemical composition and, more important, in their effects—depending upon the personality of the user and the circumstances of use. The person who misuses drugs may vary from the onetime user experimenting out of curiosity, to the chronic, heavy user who is psychologically dependent on a drug. While some types of drug misuse may be fairly apparent even to the untrained observer, other types may be so subtle they escape detection by even the expert.

Although some drug users go on to the use of more potent types of drugs, many others do not. Just why some users become dependent on particular drugs and others do not is not clearly understood. It may be related to personality development, but physiological factors also may play a role. While a physical dependency on the drug plays some role, psychological dependence appears to be more important. Physical dependence on heroin, for example, can be cured in a relatively short time. Yet the heroin addict has a very difficult time avoiding using the drug again upon discharge from treatment.

ALTERNATIVES TO DRUG USE

Youngsters who find satisfaction in other activities are less likely to find *regular* use of drugs appealing.

Many teen-agers, while attempting to appear blase or uninvolved, feel keenly the problems of our contemporary world. Therefore, opportunities for active involvement, such as work with a political party, or a program for ghetto children, are to be encouraged. While a strong interest in other activities may not deter a teen-ager from experimenting with drugs, he is less likely to adopt habitual drug use if he feels "turned on" or motivated by shared and constructive human experiences.

Adolescence is a lonely time for many youngsters. The teen-ager who is unable to find his place in some traditional group sometimes turns to drug use as a means of finding a kind of group acceptance.

Simple question-and-answer sequences about drugs are presented on the following pages. These provide the latest information on marihuana, the up-and-down drugs (amphetamines and barbiturates), LSD, and narcotics.

WHAT IS MARIHUANA?

Marihuana is a drug found in the flowering tops and leaves of the female Indian hemp plant, *cannabis sativa.*

TEEN SENSE!

The plant grows in mild climates around the world, especially in Mexico, Africa, India, and the Middle East. It also grows in the United States, where the drug is known by such names as "pot," "tea," "grass," "weed," and "Mary Jane."

The drug is made by crushing or chopping into small pieces the dried leaves and flowers of the plant. This green product usually is rolled and smoked in short cigarettes or pipes, or it is eaten mixed with food. The cigarettes are commonly known as "reefers," "joints," and "sticks." The smoke from marihuana is harsh and smells like burnt rope or dried grasses. Its sweetish odor is easily recognized.

The strength of the drug differs from place to place, depending on where and how it is grown, how it is prepared for use, and how it is stored. As a general rule the marihuana available in the United States is much weaker than the kind grown in Asia, Africa, or the Middle East.

HOW DOES THE DRUG WORK?

When smoked, marihuana quickly enters the bloodstream and acts on the brain and nervous system. It affects the user's mood and thinking, but medical science still has not discovered just how the drug works in the body, what pathway it takes to the brain, and how it produces its effects. Some scientists report that the drug accumulates in the liver. Because it may cause hallucinations when taken in very large doses, it is classed as a mild hallucinogen.

THE DRAG OF DRUGS

WHAT ARE ITS PHYSICAL EFFECTS?

The long-term physical effects of taking marihuana are not yet known because no one has done the kind of research needed to learn the results of long-term use. The more obvious physical reactions include rapid heartbeat, lowered body temperature, and sometimes reddened eyes. The drug also changes blood sugar levels, stimulates the appetite, and dehydrates the body. Users may become talkative, loud, unsteady, or drowsy, and find it hard to coordinate their movements.

WHAT ARE ITS OTHER EFFECTS?

The drug's effects on the emotions and senses vary widely, depending on the amount and strength of the marihuana used. The social setting in which it is taken and what the user expects also influence his reaction to the drug.

Usually, when smoked, the drug effect is felt quickly— about fifteen minutes after inhaling the smoke of the cigarette. Its effects can last from two to four hours. The range of effects can vary from depression to a feeling of excitement. Some users, however, experience no change of mood at all. The sense of time and distance of many users frequently becomes distorted. A minute may seem like an hour. Something near may seem far away.

HOW DOES MARIHUANA AFFECT JUDGMENT?

A person using marihuana finds it harder to make decisions that require clear thinking, and he finds himself more responsive to other people's suggestions. The drug has an adverse effect on any task that takes good reflexes

55

and thinking. For this reason it is dangerous to drive while under the influence of the drug.

WHAT ARE THE LAWS DEALING WITH MARIHUANA?

Under federal law, possession of marihuana is a misdemeanor and a first offender can be sentenced to up to a year in jail and fined up to $5,000.

The trial judge may place a first offender on conditional probation, and if the offender stays clear of trouble, the record of his arrest, trial, and conviction may be expunged (for persons under 21 years of age) or kept confidential (for persons 21 and over).

A second offense of simple possession could bring a sentence of up to two years and a fine of up to $10,000, again at the discretion of the judge.

Possession with intent to distribute, manufacture or import marihuana is a felony under federal law. A first offender can be sentenced to up to five years and a second offender up to ten years.

State laws also control the illicit use of marihuana. some state laws may be more severe than the federal laws.

WHAT ARE THE SPECIAL RISKS FOR YOUNG USERS?

Breaking the laws that deal with marihuana can have serious effects on the lives of young people. They may find their education interrupted and their future shadowed or altered by having a police record. A conviction for a felony can complicate their lives and plans at many turns. It can prevent a person from being able to enter a profession, such as medicine, law, or teaching. It can make it difficult for him to get a responsible position in business or industry. Special individual evaluation is necessary to obtain a government job. Before a teen-ager tries or sells marihuana, he should know these facts.

Experts on human growth and development point out other risks. They say that a more subtle result of drug abuse on the young person is its effect on his personality growth and development. For young people to experiment with drugs at a time when they are going through a period of many changes in their transition to adulthood is a seriously questionable practice.

"It can be especially disturbing to a young person who is already having enough of a task getting adjusted to life and establishing his values," says a National Institute of Mental Health scientist engaged in studies of young marihuana users.

Another reason for caution is the lack of scientific evidence to support statements being reported by teen-agers that the use of marihuana is "medically safe." It is hoped that research now under way may add to the little currently known about the effects of the use of marihuana.

WHAT ARE THE UP-AND-DOWN DRUGS?

These drugs are the amphetamines and barbiturates. Amphetamines, which first became available for medical use in the 1930s, are stimulants to the central nervous system and are best known for their ability to combat fatigue and sleepiness. Sometimes they are used to curb appetite in medically supervised weight-reduction programs. The most commonly used stimulants are Benzedrine, Dexedrine, and Methedrine. Slang terms for these drugs include "pep pills," "bennies," and "speed."

TEEN SENSE!
HOW DO THESE DRUGS AFFECT MOOD?

When properly prescribed by a physician, moderate doses can check fatigue and produce feelings of alertness, self-confidence, and well-being. In some people, this is followed by a letdown feeling or depression hangover. Heavier doses cause jitteriness, irritability, unclear speech, and tension. People on very large doses of amphetamines appear withdrawn, with their emotions dulled. They seem unable to organize their thinking.

HOW DANGEROUS ARE STIMULANT DRUGS?

These drugs can drive a person to do things beyond his physical endurance that leave him exhausted. Heavy doses may cause temporary mental derangement which requires hospitalization. This usually is accompanied by auditory and visual hallucinations. Abruptly withdrawing the drug from the heavy abuser can result in a deep and suicidal depression.

Long-term heavy users of the amphetamines usually are irritable and unstable and, like other heavy drug users, they show varying degrees of social, intellectual, and emotional breakdown.

Injecting "speed" (methamphetamine) into the vein may cause serum hepatitis, abcesses, and even death in the case of unaccustomed high doses. Injection of "speed" causes abnormal heart rates and may result in serious psychotic states and long-term personality disorders.

WHAT ARE SEDATIVES?

The sedatives belong to a large family of drugs manufactured for medical purposes to relax the central nervous system. Of these, the best known are the barbiturates, made from barbituric acid, which was first produced in 1846.

Barbiturates range from the short-acting, fast-starting Nembutal and Seconal to the long-acting, slow-starting Luminal and Butisol. The short-acting preparations are the ones most commonly abused. The slang terms for these include "barbs" and "goof balls."

IS BARBITURATE USE DANGEROUS?

Authorities consider the barbiturates highly dangerous when taken without medical advice and prescription. Because doctors commonly prescribe these drugs, many people mistakenly consider them safe to use freely and as they choose. They are not. Overdose can cause death or serious illness

Barbiturates distort how people see things and slow down their reactions and responses. They are an important cause of automobile accidents, especially when taken together with alcohol. Barbiturates tend to heighten the effects of alcohol.

Users may react to the drug more strongly at one time than at another. They may become confused about how many pills they have taken and die of an accidental overdose. Barbiturates are a leading cause of accidental poison deaths in the United States. They also are one of the main means people use to commit suicide.

ARE BARBITURATES ADDICTIVE?

Yes. These drugs are physically addictive. Some experts consider barbiturate addiction more difficult to cure than a narcotic dependency. The body needs increasingly higher doses to feel their effects. If the drug is withdrawn abruptly, the user suffers withdrawal sickness with cramps, nausea, delirium, and convulsions, and in some cases, sudden death. Therefore, withdrawal should take place in a hospital over a period of several weeks on gradually reduced dosages. It takes several months for the body to return to normal.

WHAT IS LSD?

A powerful man-made chemical, d-lysergic acid diethylamide, generally called LSD, was first developed in 1938 from one of the ergot alkaloids. Ergot is a fungus that grows·as a rust on rye and other cereals. LSD is so powerful that a single ounce is enough to provide 300,000 average doses.

Legally classified as a hallucinogen—a mind-affecting drug—LSD is noted mainly for producing strong and bizarre mental reactions in people, and striking distortions in their physical senses, in what and how they see, touch, smell, and hear. Except for government-approved use for research, the drug is illegal in the United States. Yet it is produced unlawfully in makeshift laboratories, and many people have taken it.

Other less known but powerful hallucinogens or psychedelic (mind-manifesting) drugs include peyote, mescaline, psilocybin, DMT, and STP.

IS LSD DANGEROUS?

Recent reports from hospitals in areas where LSD is used without close medical supervision warn of definite dangers. These dangers include:

1. Panic. Because he cannot stop the drug's action, the user may get panicky and fear that he is losing his mind.

2. Paranoia. He may become increasingly suspicious, feeling that someone is trying to harm him or control his thinking. This feeling generally lasts seventy-two hours after the drug has worn off.

3. Recurrence. Days, weeks, or even months after the individual has stopped using LSD, the things he saw and felt while on the drug may recur and make him fear he is going insane.

4. Accidental death. Because the LSD user may feel that he can fly or float in the air, he may try to leap out of a high window or from other heights and fall to his death. Or he may drive or walk in front of a moving car because he thinks he can't be harmed.

DOES LSD CAUSE MENTAL ILLNESS?

Reactions resulting from use of LSD range from great worry, panic, and deep depression, to borderline and severe mental derangement. Medical experts point out that the overwhelming worries and fears that can accompany the LSD experience are sometimes disturbing enough to cause acute and even long-lasting mental illness.

ARE THERE SPECIAL HAZARDS FOR YOUNG USERS?

The strong sensations and clash of moods the drug causes can be frightening, even for a mature person. For young people still undergoing emotional development and who seek a realistic hold on ways of solving problems and ways of living, the effects of LSD can be even more frightening and confusing. The growing brain is more vulnerable than the adult brain to all mind-altering drugs.

TEEN SENSE!

WHAT ARE NARCOTIC DRUGS?

The term narcotic refers, generally, to opium and pain-killing drugs made from opium, such as heroin, morphine, paregoric, and codeine. These and other opiates are obtained from the juice of the poppy fruit. Several synthetic drugs, such as Demerol and Dolophine, are also classed as narcotics. Opiates are widely used in medicine as pain killers. Cocaine, made from coca leaves, and marihuana, are classified legally but not chemically as narcotic drugs.

Since heroin is used by many addicts today, the following questions and answers deal mainly with heroin.

WHAT IS NARCOTIC ADDICTION?

When the abuser of a narcotic gets "hooked"—meaning addicted—his body requires repeated and larger doses of the drug, because the body develops a tolerance for the drug.

One of the signs of heroin addiction is withdrawal sickness. When the addict stops using the drug, he may sweat, shake, have chills, diarrhea, nausea, and suffer sharp abdominal and leg cramps. Modern treatments help the addict through these withdrawal stages. Science now has new evidence that the body's physical addiction may last much longer than previously believed.

There is another kind of drug dependence connected with the use of narcotics. This is known as psychological dependence. That is, taking the drug also becomes a habit for emotional reasons. For example, the addict comes to depend on the drug as a way to escape facing life.

Narcotic use can become even more of an escape than expected, because large or unexpectedly pure doses can—and not uncommonly do—result in death.

THE DRAG OF DRUGS

WHAT IS THE LIFE OF AN ADDICT LIKE?

Once on drugs, getting a continued supply becomes the main object of addicts lives. This frequently prevents the addict from continuing either his education or his job. His health often is bad. He may be sick one day from the effects of withdrawal and sick the next from an overdose. Statistics indicate the life-span of the drug-dependent individual may be drastically shortened. He usually is in trouble with his family and with the law.

DOES ADDICTION LEAD TO CRIME?

Some studies suggest that many of the known narcotic addicts have had some trouble with the law before they became addicted. Once addicted, they may become even more involved with crime because it costs so much to support the heroin habit. For example, an addict may have to spend $75 or $100 to buy his day's supply of heroin.

Most authorities agree that the addict's involvement with crime is not a direct effect of the drug itself, but turning to crime is usually the only way he has of getting that much money. His crimes are nearly always thefts or other crimes against property, and not often crimes of passion or violence.

IS IT WORTH IT?

On the basis of the evidence, the answer to the teen-age drug problem should be just about as obvious as the basic question, "Is this trip really necessary?" Don't be put down by the drag of drugs! The real question is, "Will they turn you on—or will they turn on you?"

8

Responsibility in Citizenship

Several years ago a group of students took a field trip to Washington, D.C. They visited many of the centers of both political parties. During their conversation with a distinguished senator from the Midwest, the students heard him express his gratification at seeing "Christian young people concerned about affairs of state." He told them that he had been a YMCA worker with American troops in World War I, and went on to say that he was "still eager to advance the cause of Christ."

"Well, Senator," one of the party asked, "how do you relate your Christian faith to your stand against the United Nations and all programs of foreign aid?"

The senator, an advocate of isolationism, replied more in admonition than anger. "Son," he rumbled, "I never mix religion and politics. They just don't go together!"

The conviction that religion and politics must be kept separate is not peculiar to political leaders. This conviction reflects an attitude that is common among many Americans.

RESPONSIBILITY IN CITIZENSHIP

A TOUGH QUESTION

An article in a Christian publication raises the question, Can a person be a good Christian and, at the same time, a good president of the United States? In the article the author answered, "No, he cannot." To put his nation first; to exercise effective political leadership in the practical world, would, in the author's judgment, require such serious compromise that he would end up being either a poor Christian or a poor President.

One does not have to agree with the author to appreciate the problem of compromise with which every Christian must deal. A Christian hates war, but what does he do when war involves his nation? Does he refuse to take part in it even though he knows that losing could mean the enslavement of his own people? Does he participate in it, even though his conscience tells him it is wrong to kill, because it is the lesser of two evils? I, like many teen-agers' fathers, had to make this decision. I served in the U.S. Navy for two years, then continued my education.

ANSWERS NOT EASY

The personal answers to these questions are not easy. Yet they are the kinds of questions every sincere Christian must face as a citizen. Romans 13:1-7 emphasizes the obligations the citizen owes his government. First Peter 4:12-16 reminds us that the state may make demands contrary to the Christian conscience.

In Romans 13:1-7 Paul dealt specifically with the Christian's attitude toward the state. "Let every soul be subject unto the higher powers" (Rom. 13:1). The emphasis is clear. No one can claim exemption from civil responsibility.

The nature of the subjection which Paul required in Romans 13:1-7 is not specified. But he himself repeatedly remarked that his work was possible only within the framework of established order.

In many respects, Rome was an asset to Paul's ministry. Rome afforded him the right of trial. It gave him a real measure of religious freedom in which to carry on his work. The problem came when Rome the protector became Rome the persecutor.

It is one thing to obey the state where, as in our democracy, we have some say about how, and by whom, we are to be governed, and have the legal means of changing those who govern us if we are not satisfied with their leadership. It is another thing when, as in the case of Russia, the state advocates atheism as a national policy.

FACING THE PROBLEM

What does a Christian do when, as was true when the book of Revelation was written, the state itself becomes the "beast," and the head of state a veritable anti-Christ? Even in this case, Paul would counsel obedience to the state—so far as one can conscientiously give it—on the grounds that the state is necessary to control evil, criminal forces in society.

According to Paul in Romans 13:1-2, all authority, including civil authority, is from God and ought, therefore, to be obeyed. God desires all things to be done according to law and order. Some arrangement is necessary for men to live together in an orderly manner.

RESPONSIBILITY IN CITIZENSHIP

What happens when the state makes a demand we cannot conscientiously accept? First Peter 4:12-16 helps us at this point. Peter knew from personal experience what it meant to suffer imprisonment for his faith, to live the precarious life of the persecuted. The "fiery trial" is a reality in our time. Many Christians in Nazi Germany suffered intimidation, imprisonment, and exile from their native land. Dietrich Bonhoeffer died after more than two years in a Nazi concentration camp. He had been a leader in the resistance to the rise of Hitler. For Peter, it was strange when Christians were *not* persecuted.

In our day, for Christians to be so totally conformed to the world and its course of living that they run into no trouble at all may well be an indication they have stripped their way of life of its radical, world-judging, and world-changing spirit. When the state seeks to control a right that we believe belongs to God alone, when it asks us to do something we believe is sin, then the New Testament leaves no doubt as to which loyalty takes precedence. In the words of Peter and other apostles, "We ought to obey God rather than men" (Acts 5:29).

When someone rebuked Dwight L. Moody for his active position on a local moral issue, asking him if he was not, after all, a citizen of heaven, he is said to have replied, "Indeed I am a citizen of heaven, but at the present I vote in Cook County, Illinois."

The demands in the realm of Christian citizenship are of vital importance to the world, which stands today in desperate need of a positive Christian witness. God still commissions his own to function as "the light of the world" and as "the salt of the earth."

9

Loyalty at All Costs?

Getting along in a group is part of growing into an adult. Even the urge to conform has virtue. The desire to conform helps us adjust to the realities of getting along in the world. Of all the problems the teen-ager faces, learning to handle group authority is one of the most important.

From kindergarten through college, a person advances from group to group. At each stage he is under pressure to adapt to some undefinable ideal of manhood or womanhood. A person's adjustment to the group is taken as a measure of his mental health. His popularity and the number of friends are examined as clues to his future. A child is prodded to conform to customs of his own age.

The word *conformity* has a bad connotation in modern America. People used to have the idea that the typical American was a gyroscopic, "inner-directed" person, capable of doing his own thing; the captive of no crowd. Pioneers of the Old West were such persons, their built-in "voice" directing their behavior.

Today, the average American is much more other-directed, following television commercials and magazines. Such persons live by the radar of public opinion rather than by built-in directors. They are conformers.

In which of these two groups would you put the person who seeks to be Christian? The Christian cannot think of himself *either* as an "individualist" *or* as a "conformer." He imagines neither that he carries around an infallible "voice" or "conscience," nor that he can safely settle for the motto, "Follow the crowd." Christians are called to conform to Christ and do God's work in the world. To be not conformed to the world is a Christian standard, but we are to bear witness *in* the world.

AVOID EASY SOLUTIONS

The teen-ager needs to avoid two easy solutions to the problem, "to conform or not to conform." One solution is the easy way of the "loner," who never gets wet with the tide of group life. The other is the easy way of the "grouper" who drifts with any current.

The role of the crusader does not appeal to many teen-agers. They dislike the finger-shaker who is always saying, "You ought not to be doing that." Perhaps their reasons are confused. Teen-agers may be too weak to bear even temporary separations from the affection of friends. In these days, teen-agers are under real pressures to conform.

Take a look at some options to face during these years:

Accept your friends as gifts rather than as attainments to be manipulated. Alert teen-agers, who are aware that they live by the gifts of God rather than their own works, can be sensitive to this option. They can resist the temptation to say, "Don't *you* wish you had Johnny as your friend?" or "Don't *you* wish you were a member of our club?" The Christian will not thoughtlessly increase the two-way traffic of pride and envy between the "top" cliques and the "bottom" cliques.

Be led by an attitude of inclusiveness. The appeal of the church is "Come unto me, all ye that labor and are heavy-laden." The appeal of most human groups is "Come, all ye who can measure up to our rules." Tension and contradiction always exist between the two. Teen-age groups can be rather cruel in their exclusiveness. They are not noted for forgiveness, but God *is* noted for it.

In an age of conformity to worldly standards, be a minister of reconciliation. A supreme question must be asked: "Am I continuing to conduct myself toward the exclusive group with consideration, kindness, and patient love?" Even though the teen-ager is a full-fledged member of the group, still his life is not to be under the control of the group. Jesus Christ is to be Lord of our lives, for groups can be wrong or go wrong. Group pride does not easily unbend to confess, "We are wrong, our rules are wrong, we must change." While there are many fine, wholesome groups, not all groups are healthy.

"To conform or not to conform." is not the question. The real question is, To what does a teen-ager conform? What are the guidelines to aid teen-agers in wise choices of conformity? This brings us to the rights of the teen-ager.

1. The right to an environment that is dependable, where law and order are respected. This would exclude a teen-ager's involvement in unrestrained sex expression, impulsive behavior resulting in riots, drinking intoxicants, cheating in school, breaking the barrier of "inner space" with drug kicks, vulgarity, obscenity, pornography.

2. The right to an assigned sense of personal worth. The teen-ager should not have to attract attention to get approval from parents or the group. Much of adolescent rebellion is precisely this. Acting out against societies' norms often is a cry to be noticed. The fourteen-year-old boy who prefers his basement laboratory to escorting a thirteen-year-old girl to a party may be considered "different," but if he feels the support of parents who allow him to be himself, the basement lab may fulfill more of his needs than a social life for which he is not ready.

The thirteen-year-old girl whose parents do not permit her to date may feel set apart from girls who are allowed dates. At the same time, she may be secretly relieved to have her parents make this decision for her, if like most normal thirteen-year-old girls, she already has discovered she is not yet ready for full courtship.

3. A right to be wrong occasionally without rejection. No one is perfect, and forgiveness is a virtue in the Christian faith. In exercising this freedom, the teen-ager may choose wrongly and have to accept the consequences of his choice. This in part is how growth takes place.

Group pressure has a structure like traffic on a highway. Traffic moves in certain directions governed by law. At certain street corners accidents keep on happening because of some defect: there is need for a stop sign, a traffic light, or a speed limit. So it is in our groups.

However, we can be open to the changing of rules under the impact of experience—experience which, for the Christian, always has somewhere in it the saving hand of God.

10

Developing Interpersonal Skills

He asks his mother a serious question. But before she has time to answer, he decides she doesn't know enough to answer it.

She calls her parents tyrants for restricting her telephone calls, but she brags to her friends about her parents' standards.

Who are these riddles? Like you, they are teen-agers, trying to find a place in the adult world but still not quite willing to turn loose of dependence on parents. Actions of teen-agers at any moment can be frustrating, pleasing, alarming.

THE NEED TO COMMUNICATE

Your parents and leaders wish time and again that they could understand what is going on inside your head. Often, parents are wondering what "gives" with you? Maybe you should try to communicate and to listen to one another.

In the home we are exposed to the basics of life. There we can learn to communicate, and to understand our own emotional and spiritual needs before we can really help others.

DEVELOPING INTERPERSONAL SKILLS

THE NEED TO BE RESPONSIBLE

The teen-ager is in a state of transition from childhood to adulthood. Transition times are almost always difficult. Although no typical teen-ager exists, many have similar characteristics. Some of these characteristics are exceedingly irritating to parents and leaders. For instance, the teen-ager's moodiness may frustrate others who can never be certain what the next reaction will be. A tendency to question beliefs and ideals which we once accepted without hesitancy sometimes causes others concern.

Teens are struggling to become adults and want to be treated as mature people. They desire the right to establish their own pattern of life. They may rebel at the authority of adults.

At the same time youths may confuse adults by refusing to accept responsibility. However, responsibility is a skill which can be developed. Many teen-agers demonstrate responsibility by developing interpersonal skills.

THE NEED TO SHARE

If youths can communicate and if they are responsible, does it not follow that they will want to share? Visiting a friend is one means of sharing. What are the kinds of visitation a teen-ager can do? The principles involved in visiting a sick friend and a friend in grief are discussed in this chapter.

Other kinds of visitation might include visiting in the interest of your church: inviting someone to attend, or visitation with a specific mission to present Christ to another person.

TEEN SENSE!

As persons mature we can grow in love for and understanding of the church. "Christ . . . loved the church, and gave himself for it" (Eph. 5:25). As Christ's followers, we also love the church to the extent that we give our time and energy in service. Visitation is an outreach of the church. We can help the church fulfill its purpose by ministering through visitation programs.

A purposeful visit can have as its objective enlisting a person in the learning and training program of the church. As we visit, we can explain what the church can mean for the individual, explain what study areas are discussed in the various study groups, and express sincere interest in the person's becoming part of a group.

Nothing takes the place of a personal visit to the home of a person you wish to win. Although the person visited may not respond that day to an invitation to become involved in a church group, almost everyone is impressed when someone shows enough interest to come to his home. Sending cards and letters may be good, calling on the telephone may be better, but a visit to the home is best.

WHAT TO EXPECT?

One naturally asks the question, Well, how will I be received? All of us want to be liked or accepted. I might get a cold reception some of the time, but by-and-large if I have prepared my own heart, I can count on a sensitive response. Visitors need to avoid an attitude of superiority. This attitude puts the visited people on the defensive. State briefly the purpose of your visit. Remember that you are guests in their homes and thank them for their time when you leave.

DEVELOPING INTERPERSONAL SKILLS

Above all, never become discouraged. Some teen-age prospects respond quickly. Others require a great deal of attention. No one can tell how many visits need to be made to enlist a particular prospect. It will take all of your patience to "keep on keeping on" with some persons. They may show no interest whatsoever. The tragedy is that these teen-agers, more than many others, need what the church can offer.

SKILLS IN VISITING A SICK FRIEND

Is visiting a sick friend a challenge or chore? Have you ever made or heard the remark, "I wish I enjoyed visiting in the hospital, but I don't"? For some teen-agers visiting is a real chore when it should be a challenge. Several things tend to make it a chore: finding a parking spot, learning when you arrive that the patient has just checked out, the fact that visiting can easily become routine and commonplace. Other factors, however, make visiting the sick a challenge.

A medical doctor said, "Man needs religion and particularly when he is sick." Visiting a sick friend can be a rewarding experience for you. An encouraging sign in this anxiety-ridden culture is the renewal of the church's interest in the art of healing. You may already have such an interest and want to learn how to be more effective in the ministry of healing.

VISITING THE HOSPITALIZED FRIEND

The hospital is a specialized community for giving the patient release from the demands of daily work and pressures that affect him. The hospital brings him under close supervision of doctors and nurses with tools of diagnosis and therapy immediately at hand. A wise visitor has a high regard for the doctors and nurses when he visits a patient in the hospital.

Accidents, serious illnesses, and surgery disrupt life's activities and threaten the security of persons and their families. Hospitalization creates a crisis as the ill or injured person experiences drastic limitations, suffers pain, and has to deal with strangers who minister to him. Someone familiar to the patient may be a welcomed sight.

Christian callers should remember that, while you represent God and life's central values in the sickroom, you are not absolutely necessary to the patient's recovery. In protecting your sick friend's welfare, you may be guided by the following principles:

1. A good policy in visiting is to refrain from going into any room where the door is closed, without first finding out something of the circumstances that exist behind that door.

2. A visitor should be very careful to note "No visiting" and "Isolation" signs hanging on the door.

3. A visitor should look to see if the light is on over the patient's door. If it is, do not enter until the nurse has taken care of the patient's needs. Even if the light is out, but the door is only partly ajar, knock gently before entering the room.

4. A courteous visitor never touches the patient's bed.

5. One should size up the entire situation at a glance during the process of entering the room.

6. A visitor should always let the patient take the lead in shaking hands.

7. Upon entering the room, a visitor should take a position, whether sitting or standing, in line with the patient's vision, so that the patient is not required to move around in bed.

8. A visitor must beware of letting the visit become a pathological conference. In other words, the one visiting should not make a habit of sharing his own hospital experience or that of another with the patient.

9. Helping the patient relax is important.

10. A visitor should not reveal negative emotional reactions through the voice, countenance, or manner.

11. The visitor should not make the visit too long.

12. Whispering or speaking in low tones to a nurse, to a member of the family, or to anyone else in the sickroom or near it is unwise if by the slightest chance the patient will see us or hear us.

13. As a general rule, visitors should leave when the patient's meal is delivered to his room. Or, you might say, "Well, your meal has arrived. Would you like for me to say grace with you before I go?"*

USING THE BIBLE

Determine to conduct the whole visit in a spirit of prayer. "For where two or three are gathered together in my name, there am I in the midst of them" (Matt. 18:20). Talking or laughing boisterously is unwise, since a quiet

---
*Adapted from Richard K. Young, *The Pastor's Hospital Ministry* (Broadman Press, 1954), pp. 55-60.

mood generally pervades the sickroom. Besides, laughter may be very painful for the patient being visited.

The Bible is a Christian's "royal road" to the deep levels and needs of those who are sick. The Bible furnishes many resources of strength and comfort. Like any other tool, however, it must be used effectively.

In hospital visitation the best use of the Bible is for the purpose of reassurance and comfort. Paul says, "That by steadfastness and by the encouragement of the scriptures we might have hope" (Rom. 15:4). The passages read might best be brief, applicable to the situation, well read, and preferably familiar to the patient. Some of the more appropriate passages you might read while visiting sick friends are: 2 Corinthians 12:9, Ephesians 3:14-21, Romans 8:22-28, Matthew 6:9-13, Philippians 2:5-11, Psalms 23 and 40:1-3. You may find many other comforting passages that may be read to a sick friend.

USE OF PRAYER

Prayer is an inexhaustible source of strength upon which visitors may draw. We may draw upon prayer for personal strength for ourselves as we prepare for the visit. We also may draw upon prayer as a resource to bring aid to the friend who is sick.

SKILLS IN VISITING A FRIEND IN GRIEF

Although society attempts to shield persons from the grim reality of death, we experience it both in nature and in human life. When anything is so common, we usually assume that the reaction to it will be normal. Increasingly, we are aware of the fact that unwise handling of the grief situation is causing great personal injury.

DEVELOPING INTERPERSONAL SKILLS

The writers of the Old and New Testament knew grief and dealt with it eloquently. Grief is a difficult term to define. It resembles shock, anxiety, and depression, and usually follows an acute loss or tragedy.

When the dying and those who stand with them are speechless, "the Spirit himself intercedes for us with sighs too deep for words" (Rom. 8:26).

Perhaps you have already experienced personal grief that comes when you lose a loved one. If you have not already faced it, you will. Sooner or later, everyone faces death or grief situations in life that are often more disruptive and painful than the loss imposed by death.

Some of these situations might include a person with a long-term chronic illness, or a person who is permanently handicapped. These people suffer losses much like the loss when a loved person dies. They go through the same mourning and adjusting process. Grief in death cuts with a sharp edge like a razor; grief in life cuts with the jaggedness of a saw.

Do we have to go through the experience of grief ourselves in order to comfort a friend in grief? You might ask, Do we have some practical guides for visiting the bereaved?

On occasions of suicide, accidental, or tragic deaths, no explanation will suffice for the grief-stricken. When hearts are broken, persons do not need explanations. They need the healing presence of God, who in everything "works for good with those who love him, who are called according to his purpose" (Rom. 8:28).

TEEN SENSE!

"THE GOD OF ALL COMFORT"

We often think of grief in relation to death, but grief exists in life situations. Some of these are:

1. The birth of a physically deformed or mentally defective child.

2. Persons who are misunderstood and suffer grievous injury through unjust criticism and rejection.

3. The family whose daughter marries secretly or becomes an unwed mother.

4. A social stigma attached to the family of an alcoholic or a mentally ill person.

5. Shattered courtship, a disloyal marriage partner, a dishonest business associate.

6. Events such as the loss of home, failure in school, or undesired transfer at work.

Guidance for those visiting the bereaved is available for those who would faithfully represent "the God of all comfort" (2 Cor. 1:3). Jesus' ministry with acutely bereaved persons, as with Mary and Martha of Bethany, reminds us that he readily enters into man's experiences of grief.

Most grief situations are normal. The great majority of persons meet the crisis situations of life with enough strength to go through them with a capacity they did not know they possessed. A person may say, "I don't know where I got the strength to go through this, but each day seemed to take care of itself." Often, persons can meet some of the larger crises of life with more adequacy than they can the simpler day-to-day problems.

DEVELOPING INTERPERSONAL SKILLS
THE EXPERIENCE OF GRIEF

For many persons grief is a terrifying experience. We can be of help to them. Let's take a look at this situation. A fifteen-year-old girl developed a bronchial condition. It didn't appear serious, but it developed into pneumonia. She was taken to the hospital, but in three days was dead. The only girl in the family, she had three brothers. Her parents were grief-stricken.

The pastor called and ministered in Jesus' name. A beautiful funeral service was held in the church sanctuary. The people in this family were devoted Christians, prominent in the life of the church and community. Many friends sustained them in their days of grief.

But the group who meant most to the family in comfort and encouragement was a small group of fifteen-year-old girls who were close friends of the girl who died. Their visits and encouragement, especially to the mother, were most meaningful. Never underestimate your effectiveness while visiting. If you had been a friend of this Christian girl, what might you have said to the grieving mother?

In another family tragedy, the mother is killed in an auto accident. An only child, a sixteen-year-old boy, is left. What can you do? After the initial state of shock is passed you might invite the boy along for a Coke or ask him to go camping with your family. You might invite him out with your friends for a pizza, or to attend church service with you. These may be considered small things, but they are meaningful ministries in time of need.

Also, Christian friends can listen to people who are grieving. This listening gives a catharsis of the spirit. Here, catharsis is a sharing of difficulty in which the weight of pain, grief, and disappointment is actually lightened. This catharsis can help a person restore his realistic outlook on life. It also opens the way for you to reassure and comfort the distressed person. Scripture passages can be of help in this situation.

Most of all, you can surround a person in grief with love and care.

THE NATURE OF GRIEF

You have just read how death sometimes comes into friends' lives through a catastrophe. The process through which we go in grief follows:

1. We are in a state of shock.
2. We express emotion.
3. We feel depressed and very lonely.
4. We may experience physical symptoms and distress.
5. We may become panicky.
6. We feel a sense of guilt about the loss.
7. We are filled with hostility and resentment.
8. We are unable to return to usual activities.
9. Gradually hope comes through.
10. We struggle to adjust to reality.

Extreme cases of deep depression following a tragedy may require extensive help by a minister or even a physician. Temporary hospitalization may help the person regain inner serenity and regroup his resources for confronting life again.

Paul's advice in Eph. 6:6-8 proves helpful as we minister to friends in grief.

11

Sex and Morality Today

Hugh Hefner, the son of devout Methodists, is the "king" of an $80,000,000 sexual empire of magazines, key clubs, and other *Playboy* enterprises. Once married, he is the father of two children, but is divorced. Reportedly, his present life is absorbed in his work and in fleeting relationships with first one girl and then another.

Hefner in his *Playboy* philosophy clearly believes that what is needed in the world is a greater emphasis upon sex, not the opposite. He feels that people are greatly inhibited in the area of sexual relationship and thus need more opportunities for self-expression. *Playboy* defines a young man's values, shapes his personality, sets his goals, dictates his choices, governs his decisions. *Playboy* philosophy is a substitute religion for some young people.

Other persons, like Robert Fitch, would say, "Either you control sex, or sex controls you. Needed right now are bigger and better inhibitions."

SEX SATURATED OR STARVED?

We face a confusing situation with regard to sex in our culture. On the one hand, there seems to be great frankness and freedom—a freedom which often is abused by exploitation. This has led to the characterization of our culture as "sex saturated."

At the same time, however, there is startling ignorance and misinformation, and a wistful yearning for more satisfying sexual and family life. Much marital disruption and divorce, as well as many sexual irregularities before, during, and after marriage, result from a frantic search for a more meaningful and fulfilling experience. In this sense our culture may be characterized as "sex starved."

Whether persons are sex starved or sex saturated, challenging points of view have arisen and must be dealt with. It is hardly surprising, then, that most of us are confused about the meaning, the purpose, and the function of sex in our society today. So many people have so many differing ideas about sex that we have difficulty determining just whom we should listen to. These challenging points of view have many direct and indirect effects on the way life must be lived by both single and married persons. Every thoughtful person is confronted with the necessity of understanding and managing these urgent life forces in his or her personal life in such a way that they will make the greatest contribution to personal fulfillment and society's welfare.

For the Christian this means that sex is to be understood as a good gift of God. The Bible reveals that God created sexuality with deliberate intent and blessed it (see Gen. 1:27-28). God did not make a mistake when he created male and female, although some Christians act as if he did.

But it is not enough for the Christian to understand sex as a gift from God. Sex must be expressed in ways that reveal God's purpose for that gift. The Christian is able to go beyond thinking of duties and obligations to the institution of marriage, and develop that extra measure of joy and warmth that should characterize Christian family life. How to achieve this greater abundance within the stresses and strains of today's world requires cool-headed analysis and warmhearted devotion.

Not every period in history has sung praises of sex. Many individuals, many whole societies, hated and feared human sexuality. But their loathing was a kind of upside-down way of expressing the importance of sex. It revealed the depths of their appetites and needs. John 8:1-11 records how Jesus dealt with this kind of dilemma.

Sex has always directed much of man's energy, just as it has played a large part in his fantasy. Today, although few people raise their voices openly against sex, few agree about what is good or joyful about sex—about how it should be used. Let's compare several views.

FUN AND GAMES VIEW

In the *Playboy* view sex is a marvelous indoor sport, in which every participant comes out a winner. With modern contraceptives and medicines, no one need be hurt, so the theory goes. If participants play the game fairly, no one need feel guilty. The *Playboy* attitude further purports that the pleasures of sex are so great that no one in his right mind will do without them voluntarily—unless he is mixed up by religious views. Sexual behavior is personal, and no one except the individuals involved should have anything to say about it. Young Americans have money and leisure to afford sex. They should take it with the same assurance and ease that they take all other goods and luxuries an affluent society heaps upon them.

This view is not a philosophy, but a projection of the childish wish to have what one wants, when one wants it, without effort, delay, guilt, or consequence. "Fun and Games" turns its back on public concern and grabs only for achievement of private purposes. It offers an ideal of freedom expressed as total absence of commitment.

The individual gets involved physically, period. Sex is for private use. However, *Playboy,* far from being too sexy, is really antisexual. *Playboy* dilutes and dissipates authentic sexuality by reducing sex to an accessory, by keeping it at a safe distance. For *Playboy's* man, others— especially women—are *for* him. They are his leisure accessories, his bunnies, his playthings. The success of *Playboy* illustrates the popularity of the "Fun and Games" myth—it is all right to take what you want.

THE CHRISTIAN ETHICAL VIEW

In a Christian interpretation, sex is a vital part of total existence and responsibility. True, we have always had problems of ignorance and even cruelty with regard to it. But for the Christian, sex is a gift of God to be gratefully accepted and used in harmony with his will.

The love of a married couple can turn quickly to hate if it brings an end to education, unwanted pregnancy, or a sour marriage crushed by debt and responsibility. Studies show that premarital pregnancies resulting in teen-age marriage lead to a higher than average divorce rate.

Tragically, sex also may become a weapon of abuse, turned against one's date, mate, or children. It can become an arena for the so-called battle of the sexes. It may become the source of vicious crimes, the background of weird practices of pain inflicted and received. These are known as sadomasochistic perversions.

Sex is an explosive energy in human lives that can build or destroy. When used merely for itself, sex leads to a kind of deadness. Worse than that, it can lead to cruelty, ultimately even despair. Our ancestors repressed their sexual desires for a reason. They were afraid of them. They were afraid of what might go wrong if these powers were used without discipline. They were aware that sexual excesses could lead to tragedy.

Even the world's literature does not let us forget that fact. Remember what happened to David and Bathsheba, to Antony and Cleopatra, to Don Juan and Cassanova. All of these famous stories of history and legend deal with the demonic possibilities inherent within sexual expression. And Christians, who know both the goodness of God's creation and the marks of the Fall within themselves, can easily recognize both the angelic and the devilish potentiality inherent in sex.

Without anger, without the desire to hurt, the Christian can say to a world fast becoming secular that both good and evil can come forth from sexual experience. Sexual relationship is a fragile relationship: it must be handled with care. Through it we may affirm and discover ourselves in contact with another. Or through it we may destroy ourselves.

Only in the blessed unselfconsciousness of faith and hope and love—characterized by Christian marriage—do we learn how grand beyond expression sexual relationship can be. We learn this when we let ourselves go for the sake of another. Then God lets himself go for us. In this setting marriage is what God intended it to be.

WHAT'S SO SACRED ABOUT SEX?

What is sex all about? Why did God endow with sex those whom he created in his own image?

Nowhere does the Bible say that sex is sinful. Nowhere does the Bible adopt a hush-hush attitude. The Bible is one of the frankest books in the world on the subject. It says that God made male and female and that he looked upon everything that he had made and said, "It is good."

Paul, the apostle, called the body, "the temple of the Holy Spirit," and admonished husband and wife by saying, "Do not cheat each other of normal sexual intercourse, unless of course, you both decide to abstain temporarily to make special opportunity for fasting and prayer. But afterward you should resume relations as before, or you will expose yourselves to the obvious temptation of the devil" (1 Cor. 7:5, Phillips).

SEX—SINFUL OR SACRED?

During the nineteenth century, people got the idea that the body was evil, that there was something wrong and dirty about sex. They repressed their feelings, and now we live in a period of violent reaction. Some young people express themselves by saying, "We want sexual freedom."

Sex is the foundation of marriage. Apart from marriage and parenthood, it doesn't really make sense—just as parenthood and marriage would make no sense apart from sex. The three are tied up together in one package.

SEX AND MORALITY TODAY

The main reason modern young people have a problem with sex is because, in our highly developed cultures, the age of marriage is much later than among primitive peoples. In Bible times, for instance, boys and girls often married soon after puberty. But today most youths face a stretch of five to ten years, after they have become capable of having sexual intercourse, before marrying.

The "love-in" which swept across America was an expression of this demand for freedom.

The children of Israel also held a kind of "love-in." They gathered around the golden calf at the foot of Mount Sinai, dancing and making merry. It was on this occasion that Moses came down the mountain with the Ten Commandments. One of those commandments read, "Thou shalt not commit adultery."

The Victorians, who talked a great deal about love, knew little about sex. Perhaps it is time that modern Americans, who know a great deal about sex, once again start talking about love.

It seems in every age there is a need to examine the purpose and function of sex, for sex can be sinful or sacred. Archbishop William Temple said that the reason Christians do not tell jokes about sex is because sex is holy, not because sex is dirty. Because it is holy, it is to be used as a gift from God. The Bible has many references to sex, in terms of its use and its misuse, but the assumption is that sex is essentially meaningful and good.

Sex becomes involved in our search for meaning. The desires of sex are not satisfied when sex is touted as the end-all of life. Rather they are more likely to be satisfied

TEEN SENSE!

when sex is seen in its role *under* God and not as a substitute for God. Then its pleasure is also its power for our growth as persons.

THE DRAMA OF CREATION

God endowed with sex those whom he created in his own image. In this drama of creation of male and female, the meaning of sex is revealed. In the creation story, as it is presented in the second chapter of Genesis, the creation of Adam was incomplete. As this newly-formed man looked upon all that God had made, he gave names to all of the animals. But he found there none that was like him, and he was lonely.

From what follows it is possible that his sexual nature as a man was being expressed by his loneliness. In the powerful imagery of this story, God caused Adam to fall into a deep sleep. And while Adam slept God fashioned from Adam's own body a companion for him in the form of a woman. "This is now," Adam said, "bone of my bones, and flesh of my flesh" (Gen. 2:23).

The creation story closes with the assertion, "Therefore" —because of this satisfaction of the human need for personal closeness between the sexes—"shall a man leave his father and his mother, and shall cleave unto his wife: and they shall be one flesh" (Gen. 2:24). In their cleaving to each other, they satisfy a basic human need for completion through union with another. "And the Lord God said, it is not good that the man should be alone" (Gen. 2:18).

Sex, then, is an expression of our social nature, of our outreach to another. Adam and Eve originally felt no guilt over their sexual difference. "And they were both naked, the man and his wife, and were not ashamed" (Gen. 2:25). Because husband and wife belong to each other no shame over the intimacy of marriage exists. The husband and wife express their oneness through sexual intercourse. Sex is love's personal witness in marriage. It is the most intimate form of physical communication.

From the very beginning of human life, sex has been a vital part of the totality of our existence and responsibility. Sex is a gift of God to be gratefully accepted and used for purposes in harmony with his will.

A PART OF LIFE

As God designed it, sex is an expression of the human personality. Sex is not something apart from our spirit, such as a physical plaything, but actually is a reflection of our spirit, our attitude. We are sexual beings not only when we experience specific sexual desires, but rather we are sexual beings in all that we are and all that we do. In marriage, sex is used to multiply and to unify—to procreate and to recreate.

The Bible, as we have mentioned, discloses that God chose to make man in God's own image—man on whom he could bestow his love. Then we are told that he decided to make man a sexual being. So one thing is quite clear for anyone who takes the Bible seriously—God approves of sex. If sex were, by its nature, evil or undesirable, God surely would have made us in some other form—as he could easily have done. As one of the fathers of the early church is reported to have said, "Why should we be ashamed of that which it pleased Almighty God to create?"

91

12

What Are You Looking for on a Date?

An older teen-age boy remarked, "I want my date to be a beautiful blond, deaf and dumb nymphomaniac, who h̃as no relatives and owns a liquor store." He was saying that he really did not care about the girl as a person. He wanted it done for him free of any bothersome social responsibility. Then if it didn't come off, he could blow his mind with booze. He failed to integrate sex with love and commitment. Are all young people doing that today?

A newspaper columnist, in describing a very popular girl, tried to define the secret of her charm. He decided to observe her carefully when she was on a date. He watched her enter the restaurant with her escort, saw her alert, sparkling attitude as she glanced about the room, noted her pleasant smiles and greetings to all friends, and observed, also, her well-groomed appearance.

Gradually, however, the newspaperman saw that her companion became the complete center of her interest. She listened to what he said, gave him her eyes and attention, focused her responses on him. Undoubtedly her escort was impressed, and the date was a pleasant experience.

WHAT ARE YOU LOOKING FOR ON A DATE?

Dating in these days begins at earlier ages for many young persons than was true in their parents' or grandparents' time. People used to think that dating should be delayed as long as possible. Going steady was taken much more seriously than it is today.

Today steady dating is not considered a commitment to marriage. A boy and girl may date just for the pleasure of being together, without the community expecting them to make it a permanent arrangement. Dating has become so generally accepted that a young person may go with several persons before settling upon "the one" in marriage.

The ages at which young people begin to date differ greatly, and what young people look for in a date also differs. There are, however, some guidelines which will help you distinguish between those thrills "for the moment" and those values "for a lifetime." The guide below indicates some of these thrills and values. Check those which appeal to you:

For the Moment
- (　) popularity
- (　) sharp car
- (　) good looks
- (　) life of the party
- (　) doing what comes naturally
- (　) a glib tongue and a good line

For a Lifetime
- (　) integrity
- (　) concern for others
- (　) thoughtfulness

TEEN SENSE!

(   ) respect for the body
(   ) commitment to a purpose
(   ) serious-mindedness

Boys and girls both like their dates to be good sports, but this doesn't mean that they want them to forsake their standards. It does mean that dates need to be willing and eager to have fun, be congenial, and go along with group decisions so long as they are in keeping with good taste and a basically healthy attitude toward life.

Unfortunately, many boys and girls today are looking for a momentary thrill on a date. Too many guys and gals are willing to barter an hour of excitement for a lifetime of regret. Is it worth it?

As you look over the list of "for the moment" and "for a lifetime" qualities, what do you find yourself looking for in a date? Are these qualities you want to live with for the rest of your life? Check yourself the next time you plan a date. What are you really looking for?

How can you win many friends and then one day marry one, the right one? To answer that you must start with yourself and the kind of person you are. Do others want to date you? Will anyone ever want to marry you?

CULTIVATE QUALITIES

In your date-life you will want to cultivate as many of the following qualities as possible if you would be attractive to others: consideration, generosity, friendliness, neatness, tolerance, unselfishness, optimism, sense of humor, enthusiasm, vitality.

Check yourself also for attitudes that repel other people: jealousy, irritability, rudeness, hot temper, air of

WHAT ARE YOU LOOKING FOR ON A DATE?

superiority, vulgarity, irreverence, lack of appreciation, insincerity, untidiness.

Be willing to admit your mistakes and apologize when you are wrong. Strive to be honest and straightforward, sympathetic and understanding with others, and genuinely interested in all that concerns their well-being.

During your date-life, develop your own personality through contacts with many different kinds of people. Self-restraint and self-discipline are essential. Dating can be just one physical infatuation after another, each one a little worse than the other. Love is so much more than a physical experience. Mental and emotional values are involved as well.

Ninety percent of you will win friends and eventually marry one, and you really desire to be worthy of the love you have won. You are not unusual if you have some special feeling for one particular person. At a given time, each of us tends to be drawn in a very special way to one person of the opposite sex.

Let's examine some of the advantages and disadvantages of going steady.

PLUSES OF GOING STEADY

There must be good reasons for going steady, because so many people do it. One of the reasons or advantages mentioned most frequently by young people is that they like that one person better than anyone else. When two persons discover in each other a genuine congeniality, a mutual attraction, they may prefer each other's company to that of anyone else. When they suit each other they ask, "Why date any other person?"

TEEN SENSE!

Some go steady because it saves time and money. A new girl may expect a boy to take her to interesting places and to spend money on her entertainment. But a steady may be content with a simple, inexpensive kind of date. Some steadies stimulate each other so that they actually study and work better when together. Others, however, find it almost impossible to do anything but concentrate on each other when together. For couples who are not distracted in this way, going steady may be a great saving of time and money.

In some communities a young person who does not go steady is handicapped. Some high schools are so tightly organized on a steady-couples basis that a solitary boy or girl feels left out. In such places going steady protects one from being an outsider and gives a certain social standing. A girl or boy may go steady because she or he is sure of a date. They say, "Better a second-rate date than no date."

As couples exchange confidences, they often find that they mutually encourage and stimulate each other. As soon as someone else really cares about what happens to you and listens to your troubles, your hopes, your fears, you often are encouraged to improve and to work out your problems better than before.

It is well for any couple to ask themselves this question: Is going steady good for each of us and for our particular goals? There is something not quite right about a relationship that results in a lowering of achievement and sense of responsibility.

There are advantages in going steady under certain circumstances and among certain couples. On the other hand,

WHAT ARE YOU LOOKING FOR ON A DATE?

situations exist when going steady may not be wise for a given person at a particular time.

The teen years of your life are really special. This is a time for developing taste, standards of behavior, and a meaningful set of values. It's a time to get around, meet new people, and date frequently. Every individual whose life touches yours will leave something of himself with you. In most instances, people learn more from people than they learn from books.

Even a crashing bore can teach you something. Like tolerance. The braggart and the gossip can teach you something too. The boy or girl who plays the field has a solid basis for comparison. He doesn't end up like the fly in the bottle of vinegar who thinks it's the sweetest place in the world because it's the only place he's ever been.

Those who buy date insurance by going steady pay a big premium. A free-wheeling dating pattern offers stimulating challenges and gives your personality an added dimension. Learning to associate with all kinds is essential to a well-rounded life.

MINUSES OF GOING STEADY

A major hazard of going steady is that it can become a habit. Many couples continue just because neither has the courage to break off. One boy put it like this: "I liked Nancy a lot at first. Well, I admit I talked her into doing some things she didn't think were right. Now I feel like a dirty skunk because I've lost interest. How can I ditch her without hurting her feelings?"

It may not be wise to try to go steady while you are widely separated. To promise to go steady with a friend whom you cannot see may often mean a serious halt of his activities as well as yours. When you cannot date another person because of the distance that lies between you, it often is selfishly possessive to insist that he or she not go with anyone else.

It may not be wise to continue going steady if you reach the point when you are so involved with each other that nothing else matters much any more. Some couples become so hopelessly infatuated that they cannot eat or sleep or study. When this state of affairs develops, the time has come to try to get back on an even keel. Perhaps it is wise to break off and establish other friendships.

Early marriages are sometimes blamed on unhappy homes and the general state of unrest in the world. But the truth is that most early-married couples started dating at thirteen, were going steady at fifteen, and at seventeen there was nothing exciting left, so they got married.

The bride under twenty is three times as likely to be divorced as the girl who married at twenty-two or older. At present half of all teen-age marriages end in divorce.

Early marriages do not permit the experimental contacts, the testing out of persons of the opposite sex, the utilization of courtship as preparatory to marriage.

So going steady too soon has its dangers. When it results in physical stimulation and excitation that is too frequent or too intense it has definite disadvantages. When two persons who are fond of each other spend a great deal of time together in privacy, they may begin habits that bring them to a high point of sexual excitement.

Occasionally, couples get to a place where they can enjoy each other only in their solitary love-making. Then they are apt to work each other up to a pitch of excitation they are helpless to control. When such a situation arises, it is time to call a halt before it gets out of bounds.

An important difference exists between enjoying another person in a full, rich companionship and getting so involved with him or her that you are unable to keep your attention on a variety of activities and moods. Before you get so involved that the balance is gone from your life, regain your perspective. After all, going steady ties you up, down, and in knots. It means you're supposed to be as faithful to one person as if you were married. The meeting of new boys and girls, and the growing that goes with such friendships, are not experienced by inseparable steadies.

To assume that a teen-age fellow and girl can be together hour after hour, day after day, without sexual experimentation is unrealistic. Going steady suggests that you "belong" to each other. "Belonging" implies privileges. It doesn't matter what your religious convictions are or how much self-control you have. Firm convictions and high standards are no match for raw, human instincts.

Holding hands is the first step, followed by a caress. After a while you'll run out of words. Closeness leads to necking, and necking can lead to more serious love-making. Keeping the situation under control grows tougher and tougher. Next comes the deep kiss. And then the hands get into the act. Soon you do not resist. This is not happening only to odd couples, or cheap girls and hoody boys. It happens to all kinds who find too late that reason is no match for passion.

An hour's passion is no bargain for the girl who spends five or six months in a maternity home for unwed mothers.

TEEN SENSE!

Or for a boy faced with premature family responsibilities. The trinity of the Ps: the pill, penicillin, and privacy, has not brought salvation to the area of unrestrained passion. Illegitimacy and venereal disease are on the increase among teen-agers. You may have so-called fun for the moment, but it takes more than fun for a lifetime. In other words, sex is serious, and to quote Eric Berne, a game that is played "for keeps."

The lethal quality of the "fun morality" approach to sexuality is especially clear in the research of Winston Ehrmann in his study of premarital dating behavior. Men and women play the game with different rules and different goals—in other words, a different morality.

Very often, the girl who engages in premarital sexual intercourse does so with the *hope* of a durable lasting relationship. The boy does so with the *fear* of a durable relationship. The girl has been morally schooled to have sexual relationship *only* with someone she loves. The boy has been schooled *not* to do this with someone he loves. This is a diabolical stalemate of relationship that lays the groundwork for distrust and paranoid interaction in marriage, if the couple should get married.

ETHICS OF BEHAVIOR

Sexual behavior is measured ethically not by "how far who goes with whom" as how much responsibility each is willing to take for his own behavior. Willingness, affection, and *commitment* are basic tests of meaning in sex.

One young girl said to her yet uncommitted boyfriend, "I want a man, not a boy. I am a woman, not a toy. You can go as far with me as you are willing to take responsibility for having gone, because I love you and don't want to lose you. But I am willing to lose you if you are not man enough to treat me as a woman and not a plaything, to accept as much responsibility for me as I am willing to accept for you. When you decide about these things, you can see me again and not until then."

Well, that boy grew up, just as if you'd put Vigoro in his shoes. For the young woman put the sex ethic in the realm of responsibility where it belongs.

Girls are more eager than boys to go steady, because girls are the ones on the worrying end when it comes to dating. Girls have to be chosen; they can't ask the boys. Even when a couple breaks up, the boy has the easier time. He can go right out and phone somebody else, while the girl is forced into retirement, and can only hope that some other boy soon will come along to rescue her.

The specter of old-maid status hangs over even the youngest teen-age girls, silly as it sounds. The older an unmarried man, the more desirable he is as an escort (he becomes that highly prized creature, an eligible bachelor), while an older girl who's unmarried seems to rate nothing but tea and sympathy from all the old biddies in town.

In order to avert the possibility of becoming an old maid, a girl may rush toward going steady. Ironically, it's no guarantee of anything—except, perhaps, a broken heart.

Only one type of young teen-ager should go steady. He is so dull, so unattractive, so dreary, that it's a wonder even one person would go with him. This kind of exclusiveness is best relegated to later years of courtship, as a prelude to actual engagement and marriage.

13

Outside Your Faith

Don, who came from a Baptist home, decided to marry Martha, a Roman Catholic, because "Our love will overcome any religious conflict that might arise."

Jane, an active member of her church, married Bill, who was not a Christian, because she felt she would be able to win him to Christ after their marriage.

Instances such as these where people marry outside their faith are common today. Just how important to the success of a marriage is religious harmony between the marriage partners? Is much of marriage failure today due to courtship failure? Isn't it better to match than to patch? Marriage is no reform school.

Of course, everyone agrees that marriage within one's faith does not guarantee complete success in marriage. Neither does marriage outside one's faith guarantee failure in marriage. However, religion is more important than many young persons in love are inclined to think. It may be either a source of strength or a center of conflict. To marry outside one's faith increases the possibilities of tension and conflict.

TENSIONS ARE DEEP

Tensions vary with the intensity of religious loyalty, the influence of relatives, the amount of support given religious activities, and the compromises a couple is willing to effect to solve the problems. But marriage outside of one's faith always encounters basic difficulties.

The following factors are common sources of tension in such marriages:

1. The lack of a common religious basis for ideas, purposes, and motivations.

2. The lack of resources for marital health provided by common worship and common involvement in religious activities.

3. The couple's lack of a common relationship with their children on life's deepest spiritual level.

4. The prevention of discharging the most important aspect of parental responsibility: the opportunity to bring to children the best spiritual heritage that the parent knows.

5. The possibility of one of the parties being prevented from following his conscience in regard to planning parenthood.

These problems cannot be waved away with the wand of wish. They are not products of a shallow faith or of an intolerant narrow-mindedness. They are integral problems within interfaith marriage and must be faced frankly in counting the cost of such union. Their existence has caused every major religious body in the nation to express itself as discouraging such marriages.

TEEN SENSE!

The American population is highly heterogeneous (look that word up, it's a good one), and many marriages today cross religious, national, and social lines. Marriages between persons of different religious faiths constitute a large proportion of these mixed marriages. There is psychological and spiritual realism in the biblical admonition, "Be ye not unequally yoked together. . . ." (2 Cor. 6:14).

An old proverb, reportedly of Chinese origin, holds that every man should marry the girl who lives across the street from him. This proverb is not meant to be taken literally. Rather it is a sly way of stating an important principle. What is meant is that every boy should marry a girl who comes from a similar background, whose parents are in the same general circumstances, and the couple themselves have known each other over some considerable period of time. In other words, it is a pungent way of saying, like should marry like.

If this applies to marriage it applies also to dating, for we marry those we date. It is that simple. The religious faith of the person you date is important. It may be a uniting force or a disrupting influence. It may be the prop that supports a couple during a crisis, or it may precipitate a crisis. It may make possible a profound sharing in one of the most important areas of life, or it may work against sharing. So it is important.

Young people sometimes fail to realize the importance of religion in marriage because their relatively short-time perspective does not permit a final judgment. Older teenagers often abandon religion and the church temporarily, only to return later in life, when the sober responsibilities of marriage and parenthood awaken them to a new sense of religious values. When this occurs, early training often reasserts itself. The apple seldom falls far from the tree.

Religion actually plays little part in dating, for most teens. The result is that a fellow and a girl may become emotionally involved with each other before questions of religious difference arise, since such questions assume importance in their thinking only when marriage is contemplated. Young people in love often fail to realize, also, that it is not only their religion as such that is important, but what people do in connection with it.

If religion involved only faith, entirely separate from life activities, religiously mixed marriage would present few problems. But differences in faith mean differences in practice, in attitudes toward others, foods, holidays, baptism, church loyalty, commitment to Christ. Mixed marriages also involve families with different attitudes and patterns of behavior. These can result in tugs, pressures, compromises, and conflicts as each family attempts to hold one member of a couple to the pattern which the family has set.

The Roman Catholic Church has had a pledge to which a Catholic and a non-Catholic must agree before the marriage can be performed by the priest. The non-Catholic has been asked to make the following promises:

1. That I will not interfere in the least with the free exercise of the Catholic party's religion;

2. That I will adhere to the doctrine of the sacred indissolubility of the marriage bond, so that I cannot

105

contract a second marriage while my consort is still alive, even though a civil divorce may be obtained;

3. That all children, both boys and girls, that may be born of this union shall be baptized and educated solely in the faith of the Roman Catholic Church, even in the event of the death of my Catholic consort. In case of dispute, I furthermore hereby agree fully that the custody of all children shall be given to such guardians as assure the faithful execution of this covenant and promise in the event that I cannot fulfill it myself;

4. That I will lead a married life in conformity with the teachings of the Catholic Church regarding birth control, realizing fully the attitude of the Catholic Church in this regard;

5. That no other marriage ceremony shall take place before or after this ceremony by the Catholic priest.

The only difference in the Roman Catholic party's pledge is that he agrees to do all in his power to win the non-Catholic to the Roman faith. Varied interpretations of the agreement are based on local diocesan patterns.

Although religious belief, practice, and affiliations are not the only matters to be considered in the choice of a marriage partner, they certainly should be given serious thought. Marriage outside one's faith seldom is ideal, but not always impossible. It may be like the Avis rent-a-car slogan: you have to try harder.

14

Marriage Is for the Mature

How old should a person be before he marries?

This often-asked question assumes there is a definite age at which everyone is ready for marriage. Such an assumption ignores almost all of the important factors in determining readiness for the exciting adventure of marriage.

A certain minimum age is required for marriage in all states. But age in years is seldom, if ever, the most important consideration. Actually, some people may be ready for marriage at twenty while others still may not be ready when they reach forty, and some may never be ready.

As you grow older, generally speaking, you will become more discerning and better able to choose the right person to share your life. It may take a long time. Above all, no one should marry just to get married. In reality few become as desperate as the girl in this exaggerating doggerel:

> At sweet 16, I first began
>   To ask the good Lord for a man;
> At 17, I recall,

TEEN SENSE!

I wanted someone strong and tall.
The Christmas I reached 18
I fancied someone blond and lean.
And then at 19, I was sure
I'd fall for someone more mature.
At 20, I thought I'd find
Romance with someone with a mind.
I retrogressed at 21
And found college boys most fun.
My viewpoint changed at 22,
When "one man only" was my cue.
I broke my heart at 23
And asked for someone kind to me.
Then begged at blasé 24
For anyone who wouldn't bore;
Now, Lord, that I am 25
Just send me someone who's alive!

Marriage is for mature people, and maturity includes many more considerations than the number of years lived. As a qualification for marriage, maturity involves the total personality.

Of course, no one is completely mature. But a certain level of maturity is essential if a marriage is to have a reasonable chance to become the type of satisfying relationship God intends it to be. Without maturity no marriage can really succeed, and with it few marriages will ever fail.

Maturity can be defined largely in terms of attitudes and relationships. It means being able:

1. To live happily, fully, and satisfyingly with ourselves and others.

2. To find more satisfaction in giving than receiving.

3. To use leisure time enjoyably and profitably.

4. To relate to other people in a consistent manner with mutual satisfaction and helpfulness.

5. To deal capably with the stresses of life, to tolerate the anxieties that inevitably come our way and to endure the frustrations that assail us.

Emotional maturity does not mean perfection. All of us have faults and weaknesses. Maturity means the control of these faults to the best of one's ability. It also means the acceptance of these faults in other people and the ability to forgive such faults with love. When we love maturely, we do not cherish illusions about our loved one. Rather, we love with honesty and tolerance.

A mature person is one who has the capacity to love somebody else. Physical attraction will have a definite place in this love, but it must not predominate. Respect, admiration, acceptance of the other person as he really is —all of these factors must be a part of genuine love.

Teen-agers should prepare themselves for marriage and adults should help them prepare. When a teen-ager realizes the responsibilities of marriage, he is likely to become more interested in making adequate preparation for marriage than he is in getting married immediately.

All persons wish to be mature, but few may know how to go about achieving maturity. Certain suggestions, put into practice, can go a long way toward helping youths mature.

1. *Talk Out Your Problems.* If something is disturbing you, talk it out, don't bottle it up. The adage holds true

that honest confession is good for the soul. Find some level-headed, understanding person and share your burden with him. Prayer, sharing our concerns with God, may help us more realistically evaluate our situations.

2. *Channel Your Hostility.* Everyone gets angry. Jesus was indignant at the money changers in the temple. The expression of anger is not condemned in the biblical account except as it is done apart from the covenant of forgiveness and reconciliation. The Apostle Paul recognized that anger was inevitable, but that quick reconciliation was necessary to vital living. "Be angry but do not sin; do not let the sun go down on your anger" (Eph. 4:26).

On one occasion Jesus said, "If you are offering your gift at the altar, and there remember that your brother has something against you, leave your gift there before the altar and go; first be reconciled to your brother, and then come and offer your gift" (Matt. 5:23-24). This normal way of handling hostility in the covenant of love also is coupled with the experience of tenderheartedness and forgiveness.

3. *Take a Break.* Escape is no permanent solution to life's problems. But it is perfectly realistic and healthy to escape long enough to recover breath and balance, enabling us to take an objective look at our subjective problems. Making ourselves stand there and suffer is a form of self-punishment, not a way to solve a problem. There are a few simple things that may help us catch our emotional breath: read a good book, participate in wholesome recreation, do something for others. These may prepare us to come back and deal with our difficulties when we are more composed.

4. *Admit the Possibility of Error.* Some people can not lose an argument. These people are not happy with their "imagined psychological maturity"—as psychologists would describe it, or with their self-righteousness. To them life is a hard battle with a short stick and they dare not stop swinging the stick. It is far better to let "the defense rest" occasionally.

5. *Don't Play God.* Remember your finitude. The Apostle Paul reminds us that "We have this treasure in earthen vessels, to show that the transcendent power belongs to God and not to us" (2 Cor. 4:7). And he urges us not to think more highly of ourselves than we ought to think, "But to think with sober judgment, each according to the measure of faith which God has assigned him" (Rom. 12:3).

Jesus asked, in this connection, "Which of you by being anxious can add one cubit to his span of life?" (Matt. 6:27). Some people expect too much from themselves, and get into a constant state of anxiety and frustration because they think they are not achieving as much as they should. They try for perfection in everything. Admirable as this ideal is, it is an open invitation to failure, for no one can be perfect in everything. Decide which things you do well and put your major effort and interest into these.

6. *Curb Criticism.* Jesus, with penetrating insight, said, "Judge not, that you be not judged. For with the judgment you pronounce you will be judged" (Matt. 7:1-2). We all know people who consistently criticize others for their troubles or shortcomings. Others believe they never get a square deal. These people are using a defense mechan-

ism called *projection*—attributing to others wishes or faults that they will not claim as their own.

Often, criticism reveals more about the person doing the criticizing than the person being criticized. Remember, each person has his own virtues, his own shortcomings, his own values, his own right to develop as an individual. Instead of being critical about the other person's behavior, search out the good points and help him to develop them. This will give both of you satisfaction, and help you to gain a better perspective on yourself as well. "Be kind," said Ian McLaren, "for nearly everyone you meet is fighting a hard battle."

7. *Participate in the Life and Work of Your Church.* The church and the Christian faith help us assess our allegiances and clarify our loyalties in order that there be no idolatry to minor values. The church as a fellowship of the concerned can be a meaningful buffer in the turbulent teen years. Group acceptance and approval are needed by every person.

Underlying these seven practical suggestions is a basic philosophy fundamental to mature living. That is the philosophy of faith: faith in ourselves; faith in others; faith in God. These three will have everything to do with your being able to live the abundant life which Christ gives. Maturity depends not upon being free of problems, but upon facing and solving them adequately—with the resources God so generously provides.